MW00770159

ECORSE

MICHIGAN

KATHY COVERT WARNES

ECORSE

MICHIGAN

A BRIEF HISTORY

Charleston London

THE
History
PRESS

Published by The History Press
Charleston, SC 29403
www.historypress.net

Copyright © 2009 by Kathy Covert Warnes
All rights reserved

First published 2009

Manufactured in the United States

ISBN 978.1.59629.803.3

Library of Congress Cataloging-in-Publication Data

Warnes, Kathy.
Ecorse, Michigan : a brief history / Kathy Covert Warnes.
p. cm.
Includes bibliographical references and index.
ISBN 978-1-59629-803-3 (alk. paper)
1. Ecorse (Mich.)--History. 2. Ecorse (Mich.)--Biography. I. Title.
F574.E35W37 2009
977.4'33--dc22
2009026249

Notice: The information in this book is true and complete to the best of our knowledge. It is offered without guarantee on the part of the author or The History Press. The author and The History Press disclaim all liability in connection with the use of this book.

All rights reserved. No part of this book may be reproduced or transmitted in any form whatsoever without prior written permission from the publisher except in the case of brief quotations embodied in critical articles and reviews.

CONTENTS

ACKNOWLEDGEMENTS

Morris "Sandy" Blakeman, who took most of the photographs in this book, loved Ecorse and worked to improve his adopted hometown. Born in Circleville, Ohio, he came to Ecorse when he was a young man to work at Great Lakes Steel. After fighting in Normandy and throughout the rest of Europe in World War II, he returned to Ecorse with his Scottish bride, Mary, whom he had met and married in England in 1943. Sandy worked at Loveland's Drugstore in Ecorse for a time and eventually branched out into real estate and photography. He served as one of the official photographers for Ecorse for many years and took many of the wedding photographs for Ecorse couples, as well as official photographs for the city. I thank him for his loving and dutiful work on behalf of Ecorse. Joie Manning, Nancy Mitchell, Mary Blakeman and Jeanette Richter also deserve thanks and acknowledgements for their contributions to this Ecorse history. Sandy Blakeman, John Duguay, Bill Manning and John Reidy deserve posthumous recognition for their inspiration and contributions.

CHAPTER 1

ALONG THE RIVERS ECORSE AND DETROIT

Some anthropologists and historians estimate that at least seven thousand years ago the Huron (later called Wyandot) and Potawatomi tribes owned and occupied the territory on both sides of the Ecorse and Detroit Rivers. French priests and voyageurs first explored the Detroit and Ecorse Rivers, and before the American Revolution, the French flag floated over the Down River area, which was then a part of the province of Quebec. Ecorse is bounded on two sides by Ecorse Creek, which at this earlier period enjoyed the romantic name of La Riviere aux Ecorces. The word "ecorces" is the French word for bark, and the French translation of La Riviere aux Ecorces is "the river of bark." The name comes from the fact that Huron Indians buried their chiefs near the sandbanks of this stream after wrapping the bodies in the birch bark. Early Down River residents reading the deeds to their properties often found the first pages written in French and even some pages with drawings of fish, turtles or birds. These were signatures of the original owners, the Potawatomi and Wyandot Indians.

In 1701, Antoine Cadillac landed in what is now Detroit and established French "ribbon farms" along the Detroit River as far as present-day Monroe, Michigan. Because water transportation was essential in these early times of dirt trails and dense forests, every farmer wanted to own land rights on the Detroit River and near Fort Pontchartrain. Cadillac gave each farmer land on the riverfront, which followed the shoreline for two hundred to one thousand feet and extended from the Detroit River back two to three miles. (They were called ribbon farms because the lands were long and narrow.) These farms lined both sides of the Detroit River from Ecorse to Lake St. Clair. The farmers used their canoes on the Ecorse River, River Rouge and the Detroit River to visit other farmers and friends in Fort Pontchartrain (early Detroit) and to take their farm produce and furs to market. The proximity of the

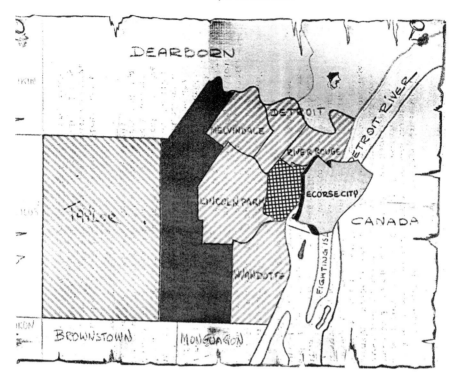

Ecorse Township was created in 1827 with an area of fifty-four square miles. A post office, always named Ecorse, opened on October 29, with Daniel Goodell as the first postmaster.

farms to the fort provided protection and allowed the farmers crucial access to the rivers, which provided them with a transportation and communication highway. Many of the descendants of the early settlers trace their origins to this strip of ribbon farms.

The French ruled the territory for the next fifty-nine years. Beginning about 1707, Cadillac granted land on both sides of the Detroit River to French settlers who wanted to farm. The 1707 date is the organization date of Ecorse, even though it didn't become an incorporated village until 1903 and a city until 1942. A few Down River historians even argue that in 1699, two years before the founding of Detroit, a Pottawatomie chief scratched his mark on papers granting the first French settlers claim to land at the mouth of the Riviere aux Ecorces. Either date establishes Ecorse as the oldest Down River community.

The early French settlers can trace their land titles back to 1746, some forty-three years before George Washington became the first president of the brand new country called the United States of America. In the next decades,

Ecorse became a city in 1942 and has a total area of 3.6 square miles, consisting of 2.7 square miles of land and 0.9 of water. *Courtesy John Duguay.*

the French and the British disputed ownership of the Great Lakes and Ohio country. Chief Pontiac of the Ottawa and his warriors unsuccessfully plotted the capture of Fort Detroit from their campground on the Riviere de Ecorces, and the Treaty of Paris in 1763 settled the Seven Years' War in favor of the British.

Pierre LeBlanc, who would later settle in Ecorse, was one of the first Frenchmen to travel to the area, arriving in 1790 for the Hudson Bay Company. Fur trading comprised most of the business in this western country at this time and created Native American, French and British capitalists. Hunting fur-bearing animals like beaver and muskrat, preparing their furs for market and transporting them to Montreal provided much of the impetus for exploration and settlement along the straits and along the Ecorse River. Trade was carried on between Montreal and the upper country by canoes and bateaux. Canoes loaded at Montreal were brought to Detroit either over the Ottawa River coming down through Georgian Bay or through the Niagara route over Lakes Ontario and Erie. The Niagara Route was easier because it had one portage at Niagara Falls while the Ottawa Route had at least thirty portages.

Since French and other white women were scarce in this frontier settlement, Pierre married a Fox Indian woman and established a homestead farm on what is now West Jefferson near the Detroit River. When a French trapper took an Indian wife, his marriage helped him survive Indian attacks or other trouble with the warriors still numerous in the Down River area. The LeBlancs established themselves as sturdy farmers and trappers, trading with the Indians and maintaining a good relationship with them. The Detroit River and Ecorse Creek figured prominently in the lives of the LeBlanc family.

Pierre and his Indian wife had a son, whom they named Pierre, born in 1820 in a log house on the old family farm. This log house served as a place of worship for the early Catholics, and for many years Mass was held within its rustic walls. Early in his life, the second Pierre revealed his sturdy French stock and Indian blood. He was a constable when he was only twenty years old, and for many years he was a highway commissioner, laying out many of the first roads in the southeastern part of Michigan. Pierre's generation of frontier settlers depended mainly on trapping, hunting and fishing for a living, and Pierre was credited with killing the last deer in Ecorse. His uncle, Joe Cicotte, killed the last bear, bagging the animal where the offices of the Michigan Alkali Company once stood. The two Pierres also made pitfalls for wolves because the animals so often raided the sheep on which the farmers depended for wool and meat. Using mutton for bait, the Pierres, father and son, lured the wolves into a deer pit from which they couldn't escape, leaving the trappers to shoot them with six-foot muskets.

In 1850, the LeBlancs built a new house to replace the old log cabin, and Pierre's son, Frank X. LeBlanc, was born in that house. Through his years of growing up on the LeBlanc farm near the river, Frank X. collected many souvenirs of his family's early days in Ecorse and the vicinity. Among them was a receipt given to his grandfather Pierre by Peter Godfroy, a merchant who was the sole survivor of the Indian massacre at Frenchtown in Monroe in which the entire garrison and all the settlers within the fort (except Godfroy) were tomahawked. Although yellowed and faded, the receipt for goods that LeBlanc had purchased from Godfroy was still legible. Another valuable record was a tax statement that the sheriff of Wayne County sent to Pierre LeBlanc in July 1824. The statement requested LeBlanc to pay the $2.03 he owed in taxes!

The Campau family might have originated in LaRochelle, France, before early Campaus immigrated to Canada and then Detroit. A June 1750 document describes Jacques Campau Sr. as "a habitant living at Detroit." *The History of Wayne County* notes that Jacques' children were "respectable citizens, honest and industrious people who left good names behind them when they died."

Along the Rivers Ecorse and Detroit

One documentary record states that the earliest setter in the territory that was to become Ecorse Township was Pierre Michael Campau in 1795, but the early private records of the Labadie family show that Labadies settled near the mouth of the Ecorse River in 1764. L. Campau, writing in 1818, said that the first American farmers in the Detroit area originated from two groups. Some were Indian prisoners taken during the Revolutionary War who remained behind after the peace, and the other group were Englishmen who came when the English assumed control of Detroit and remained after the Revolutionary War as Americans. In the later years of the seventeenth century and in the early 1800s, many other French settlers established themselves on or near the Ecorse River, including the Salliotte, Cicotte, Champaign, LeBlanc, LeDuc, Baby, Bourassa, Riopelle and Rousseau families. An 1876 map of "Ecorce" reveals the names of settlers along the branches of the Ecorse River, including Riopelle, Montie, Bondie, Campau, Cicotte, Champaign, LeBlanc and Labadie. English settlers in smaller numbers also came to the territory. When John Quincy Adams was sixth president of the United States, the Michigan Territory was divided into townships. The United States Congressional Ordinance established the Northwest Territory and set forth procedures for land measurement and recognized the old French land grants.

Pierre St. Cosme is another important name in the early history of Ecorse. On July 1, 1776, three days before America released its Declaration of Independence, "the Poutououatamis Nation awarded Pierre Cosme and Amable and Dominique St. Cosme, his sons, a grant of land for a consideration of 'Love and Affection.' The deed, dated July 1, 1776, granted to Pierre St. Cosme and his children land fronting the Detroit River and the River Ecorces toward Wyandotte and Turkey Island [or Fighting Island] opposite the River Ecorse." The land included all of the territory from what is now Southfield Road to the River Raisin in what is now Monroe. The original settlers of the region received their deeds of property from the heirs or assigns of Pierre St. Cosme. The first road in the region was constructed on land granted to the township of Ecorse by the St. Cosme line. Years later, the name was changed to State Street, and still later to Southfield Road.

A different set of documents contend that the Labadie family first settled in what was later to become Ecorse Township in 1764. If the witnesses appearing in records of property right litigation in 1821 are correct, then Pierre Michele Campau and Jean Baptiste Salliot were the first to cultivate farms along the Detroit riverfront, and the date of the earliest settlement is given as 1814. Other early settlers in Ecorse were J.B. Rousson, Louis Bourassa, Joseph Bondie, J.B. LeBeau, Pierre LeBlanc, Gabriel Godfroy and Jonathon Scheffelin.

Family tradition says that the first Goodell in America was Robert Goodell, who immigrated to Salem, Massachusetts, in 1634 from England, to which the family had fled in the mid-1500s to escape religious persecution in their native France. Tradition also has it that these early French Huguenots changed the spelling from Goodelle to Goodell. Elijah Goodell, his wife Achsah (Pickert) and their family moved from the Mohawk Valley in New York to Canada. In the 1790s, the British government passed laws requiring all residents of Canada to swear an oath of allegiance to the Crown. Elijah could not swear allegiance to a country that he had fought, so he fled with his family to the United States and settled on Grosse Ile in 1799. The Goodells were French Huguenots, and the name is spelled Goodelle in many of the old records. They had twelve children—eight sons and four daughters. All of their children came to Michigan Territory with them except Andrew, the oldest son, who remained in the Mohawk Valley, where his descendants still live today.

In the early 1800s, Elijah brought his family to the pioneer settlement of Ecorse because the federal government had awarded him a land grant for his service in the Revolutionary War. His land lay between the Detroit River and present-day Jefferson Avenue, between what is now Salliotte and Benson Streets. The settlement of Ecorse consisted chiefly of French Catholics, so the Goodell family settled in with two differences: they were French Protestants, and they were the only English-speaking family in the area. Elijah quickly overcame these handicaps and assumed a position of leadership in the community. He served for many years as agent in charge of Indian affairs over a large area between Detroit and Fort Mackinac.

The Goodell's log cabin home, one of the largest in Ecorse, served as a social, civic and religious meeting place. Tradition has it that the Reverend Father Gabriel Richard, on his monthly visits to the Down River area, sang Mass in the cabin's large kitchen. If this story is true, it is even more remarkable because the Goodells themselves were Protestant. The kitchen itself, with its original thick log walls, survived in a house built around it on Alexander Court, between Benson and Goodell, not far from the spot on which Goodell built his first log cabin home. Elijah died in 1820.

Daniel Goodell, one of Elijah's eight sons, was born in New York in 1794. He served as a private in Major Witherell's Detachment, Michigan Volunteers, and in the militia in the War of 1812. Daniel was captured when General Hull surrendered Fort Detroit to the British on August 16, 1812. For military service in the War of 1812, Daniel Goodell received Land Warrant 2225 for 160 acres of land in Wisconsin, but he didn't move there. Many warranty deeds, promissory notes and similar legal papers that were executed in Ecorse Township in the 1840s through the 1860s bear Daniel's signature as a witness. A terse entry in the Goodell family genealogy reveals Ecorse's stake in the War of 1812. Sergeant John Goodell was killed in Amherstburg, Ontario, during the war.

Within the historical framework of the War of 1812, Ecorse and its rivers and connecting lakes often became centers of the conflict. The United States and Great Britain were the main combatants in the War of 1812, but the war was also a civil war in the sense that it pitted Indian nations, as well as different sections of the United States, against one another. In a figurative and too often literal sense, it made the United States and Canada train their rifle sights on each other across their common border, especially along the vital Detroit River artery, and it fueled the ambitions of many Americans to invade and annex Canada. Canadians and Americans still vied for the allegiance of the Indian tribes and for their land.

The Indian headquarters at Fort Amherstburg had an important influence on the Detroit River. Experienced and resourceful people such as Simon Girty, Matthew Elliott and Alexander McKee, veterans of the Revolutionary War, led the Amherstburg Indian Department, which sought the allegiance of the tribes in the Northwestern Territories and their loyalty in case of a war with America. The efforts of Girty, Elliott and McKee and other Indian Agents made Fort Amherstburg a supply center for the Indian tribes and their main source of food, cloth, tools, weapons and ammunition. The success of these Indian agents just across the river irritated Americans who felt that the Amherstburg Indian Department was interfering with internal American affairs. To many Americans, this interference meant war with the British. As the year 1811 drew to a close, the Indians of the Great Lakes region were increasingly armed and restless, due in large part to the Amherstburg Indian Department.

On July 5, 1812, General Hull and his army arrived in Detroit, and on July 12 General Hull and his forces crossed the Detroit River between Detroit and Sandwich above Fort Amherstburg and marched into Upper Canada. General Hull issued a proclamation assuring Canadians that "I come to protect not to injure you." The American army was twice the size of the British detachment, so when the Essex Militia stationed in Sandwich met them at a bridge over the River Canard on July 16, the Americans pushed the British back. The British withdrew to Amherstburg, but General Hull worried about his supply lines and lack of heavy artillery to batter Fort Amherstburg, so he didn't follow up his victory. The Americans set up camp at Francois Baby's farm on the Detroit River, and General Hull issued a proclamation that convinced about five hundred Canadian militiamen to desert. The Americans followed the British toward Amherstburg, but Canadian ships anchored near the mouth of the River Canard and British troops and Indians stopped the Americans from advancing to Amherstburg. General Hull wanted to use his large guns against Fort Malden at Amherstburg, so he delayed the attack for two weeks while the guns were being readied. On July 29, he heard that the British had captured the fur trading post at Fort Mackinac and immediately worried that the northern Indians would come south to help the British.

The British were not yet strong enough to push the Americans off Canadian soil, so they focused their military efforts against Hull's supply lines. Groups of British regulars, Canadian militia and Indians fanned out from Fort Amherstburg, jeopardizing American communication and supply lines on the west bank of the Detroit River. They attacked two key American supply lines, and in early August 1812, Captain Henry Brush led an American relief column from the River Raisin in Monroe to Detroit, bringing in cattle and other supplies to General Hull's army. Captain Brush sent a messenger to General Hull, who was encamped at the Canadian town of Sandwich, present-day Windsor, Ontario. The message advised him that Shawnee chief Tecumseh and some of his warriors had crossed the Detroit River and advanced to the vicinity of Brownstown and that British regulars were probably escorting and advising him.

Captain Brush asked General Hull to send him troops from Detroit to protect his supply column, and on August 4, 1812, Major Thomas Van Horne, commander, and two hundred Ohio militia marched south down the road that they had just cut through the Black Swamp to bring supplies to Detroit. As Major Van Horne and his men crossed Brownstown Creek, three miles north of the village, Tecumseh and twenty-four of his Indian combatants ambushed one of the supply columns. Amidst the confusion of crackling rifles, flitting shadows and revolving battle lines, the Americans began to retreat. The Indians chased the Americans as far as the Ecorse River before they melted into the woods, and the Americans returned to Detroit.

The American casualties in the Battle of Brownstown included eighteen men killed, twelve wounded and seventy missing. The Indians lost one chief. The skirmish outside of Brownstown did not turn the tide of the war, but it did reveal that the American supply line to Ohio was not secure and convinced General Hull that the British and Indian forces outnumbered him, a conviction that would ultimately lead to the surrender of Detroit to the British. After two more years of hard-fought campaigns, the United States finally battered the British to a draw, and both sides endorsed the Treaty of Paris, ending the war. After the Treaty of Paris, the French and English settlers in Ecorse resumed the task of carving homes out of the Michigan wilderness.

CHAPTER 2

FOUNDING FAMILIES

On August 10, 1818, Governor Lewis Cass commissioned Daniel Goodell as lieutenant in the militia of the Territory of Michigan. He married Susanne Baron, daughter of Antoine Baron, on July 18, 1820. Daniel Goodell's daughter, Maria, married James Perry. Peter Perry, his father, had fought under General Henry Proctor with the Second Regiment, Essex Militia, Canadian army, and settled on a farm at present-day Goddard and Biddle with his wife Elizabeth (Barrien). Their son, James, found it easy to court Maria Goodell because the Goodells' fifty-five-acre farm was north of the Perry farm and about half a mile south of Ecorse Creek.

When patriarch Elijah Goodell died in 1820, he was buried in a small family graveyard on his property near the Detroit River. Eventually, his gravestone was moved to Alexander Court, between Benson and Goodell Streets, near the spot where he had built his first log cabin home. For many years, motorists traveling busy Jefferson Avenue passed his gravestone nestled against an ivy-covered fence without knowing that it was there. Most Ecorse residents didn't know it was there. In 1973, Elijah's descendant, Dr. Blanche E. Goodell, retired Wayne State University professor, died. Members of her family honored her request to have the gravestone moved to Detroit's historic Elmwood Cemetery. Despite its great age, the lettering on Elijah Goodell's gravestone records his death in 1820 and that of his son, Sergeant John Goodell, who was killed in Amherstburg, Ontario, during the War of 1812.

Their descendant, Dr. Blanche Goodell, taught in the Ecorse public school system in 1915 and 1916 and was a faculty member at River Rouge High School from 1919 to 1921. Also in 1921 she began her years of service to Wayne State University and was head of the Spanish Department at the time of her retirement in 1961. Despite the fact that she served in several Detroit community and civic organizations, including the Detroit

Historical Society, Dr. Goodell continued to live in the community in which her ancestors settled. The Goodell name survives on schools and streets in several communities.

According to Detroit historian Friend Palmer, the Cicotte family has a 150-year-old tradition in Ecorse, and Francois X. Cicotte was "a fine specimen of the early Frenchman possessing that rare charm of manner which seemed a peculiar legacy to these descendants of the first pioneers."

In 1812, General William Hull commissioned Francois Cicotte as captain of a small company composed of men who were experienced in the toils, dangers and challenges of frontier life and noted for their discipline and courage. After Colonel Winchester was defeated at the River Raisin, an Indian chief brought Dr. Brown, a Kentuckian, to Francois Cicotte to sell as a prize. The Indian sold Dr. Brown for $100, and Captain Cicotte paid him that sum. Afterward, Dr. Brown visited Cicotte when he returned to Detroit with General William Henry Harrison's army.

After the Battle of the River Raisin, a few teams were sent down to collect the bodies and effects of the dead soldiers. Captain Francois Cicotte and his brother, Jean G., traveled to Monroe, each with a pony and a traineau—a peculiar kind of sledge, useful for traveling in deep snow. Arriving at the River Raisin, they saw unburied bodies of the fallen soldiers and their Indian allies. Cutting a wagonload of thorn brush, they put the bodies in the back of the traineau, covered them with brush and started on the return trip to Detroit. Captain Cicotte happened to be driving the team in front, and as they approached the territory of Blue Jacket (a noted Indian chief) a little below Trenton, he noticed a robust, strong-looking young white man standing by a tree. As Captain Cicotte sat wondering what the young man was doing in the woods, he heard the crackling of two rifles, and the young man fell. The balls from the Indian rifles passed through his heart, and he fell to the ground, gasped and died. The Indians appeared, cut off his feet and carried them triumphantly away. The white man had been taken prisoner, escaped and gotten confused in the deep forest, and the pursuing Indians had overtaken him.

A few days later, Captain Cicotte and his company were ordered to scour the banks of the River Rouge and the River Ecorse several miles upstream to drive off the Indians and protect the farmers and trappers along its banks. Arriving at old Francis Chovan's farm, he spotted an Indian escaping into the woods. One of the soldiers shot the Indian, who tumbled head over heels and then sprang to his feet and ran off. When the scouts approached the spot, they discovered that the Indian's blankets had deflected the musket ball, allowing the warrior's escape.

Founding Families

One of Francois Cicotte's descendants, who also went by the name of Captain Cicotte, loved horses and horse racing, and he and Lieutenant U.S. Grant, Barney Campau, Major Bob Forsythe and many others used to liven up the winter silence by racing down Jefferson Avenue from the bridge and racing on the River Rouge when icy conditions permitted. Cicotte descendants Adeline LeBlanc Cicotte, who was born in 1847, is buried in St. Francis Xavier Cemetery (Ecorse Cemetry), as are Charles, Clara, Edward Elizabeth, Elmer, Isaac, Joseph, Josie, Lillie, Louis, Mathilda and Susan Cicotte.

Even though the cemetery wasn't blessed until 1882, church records indicate that the first burial in St. Francis Xavier Cemetery took place in 1848 when Charlotte Cook, wife of Moses Salliotte, was laid to rest on September 7. Only thirty-three years old when she died, Charlotte was born in Yorkshire, England. Moses Salliotte also rests nearby. His epitaph reveals that he died on March 9, 1892, at the age of eighty-five. He was born in Ecorse and was one of the earliest settlers in the village.

The Bondie (or Bondy) name is also prominent in early Ecorse. Teresa Saliot was the daughter of John Saliot and Mary Magdelene Jourdain. She was born on September 9, 1782, and she married Dennis Bondie, who was born on January 26, 1779, in Sandwich, Ontario. Teresa's sons and daughters married into the Navarre and LeBlanc families.

Another early settler, William Nowlin, writes about everyday life on the north branch of the River Ecorse in his account of pioneer life in the wilderness of Michigan, *The Bark Covered House*. The oldest of five Nowlin children, William journeyed to Michigan with his parents, John and Melinda, from what he considered civilized life in New York and left a graphic, detailed account of his life in early Ecorse Township near present-day Taylor. William was born on September 25, 1821, and family talk about migrating to Michigan began about 1832, with the family making the move to Michigan in 1833–34. They boarded the steamer *Michigan* and arrived in Detroit in the spring of 1834. From Detroit, William and his father John walked with guns on their shoulders to their brand-new farm one mile south of Dearborn. The next day, his mother Melinda and the rest of the family came to the homestead, and in one week, John Nowlin had built a bark-covered house for his family.

John Nowlin bought an additional eighty acres of land, and the north branch of the River Ecorse, flowing east, ran through his land. Beech, hard maple, basswood, oak and hickory trees grew on the land on both sides of the creek, and ash and elm trees flourished farther back from the creek. The Nowlin family, especially William, immediately began to make maple sugar.

Over the next few years, the Nowlins slowly acquired new neighbors up and down the creek.

Joseph Pardee was one of the Nowlins' neighbors. He came to Michigan in the fall of 1833, claimed his land and built the first log house on the Ecorse River west of the French settlement at its mouth on the Detroit River. According to William Nowlin, Pardee possessed a strong mind, an iron will and a determination to leave his mark on the new land. Pardee cleared his land and carved out an extensive farm. When he died in 1859 at the age of eighty-one, he left his family in excellent circumstances.

Other Nowlin neighbors besides Joseph Pardee who came to settle along and near the Ecorse in the fall of 1833 were Asa Blare, who came in the fall of 1834, and Henry Travis, who came in the summer of 1835. George Purdy came in the fall of 1835, and Elijah Lord, about 1837 or 1838. In 1875, when William Nowlin wrote his book, George Purdy still lived on the Ecorse River and owned a good farm. William marveled at how quickly the land along the river became settled. He could stand by the Nowlin house, look to the west and see Joseph Pardee's house and the smoke from his chimney. He could even see Pardee and his sons when they came out of the house to do their morning chores. He could look to the east and see the house of Asa Blare that adjoined the Nowlin land. As William put it, "The light of civilization was beginning to dawn upon us."

Squire Goodell (probably Elijah Goodell) was another Nowlin family friend. William wrote about traveling through the woods to see Squire Goodell, who lived near the Detroit River. William asked Goodell to fill out papers that would enable him to collect the state bounty on wolves. William received the bounty but didn't mention catching any wolves. He reported seeing many of them in the woods and hearing them so often at night "that we became familiar with them."

In the spring after the ice broke up on the Ecorse River, pike or pickerel came up from the Detroit River in large numbers, and William and his neighbors went fishing. The water ran high in the creek, often overflowing its banks. In William Nowlin's words, "The Ecorse appeared like quite a river." But William and his friends conquered the Ecorse. They made a canoe of a white wood log and launched it on the river. Sometimes they went fishing in the canoe, but when they fished from the canoe, William always had to take a friend along, because the pickerel lay in shallow water where old grass grew. By scrutinizing the surface of the water, William could see the small ripples that the fish made with their fins while they were swimming. The person in the back end of the canoe poled carefully toward the place where William saw the ripples, and when they reached the fish they speared or shot them.

Founding Families

The fish ran up the Ecorse River two or three weeks every spring, and the fish that didn't get caught swam back into the Detroit River. William's father John made a pike net with two sections. By the time the fish were running back into the Detroit River, the water had settled into the bed of the creek. John Nowlin set his net in the Ecorse riverbed, stretched the sections across the river and staked them snugly. The fish ran up the Ecorse River at night, and in the evening John would set his net. The next morning, he would have a splendid catch of fish. William helped his father salt some of the fish that they couldn't eat to preserve them for summer meals.

William Nolin eventually married and worked to establish his own claim along the Ecorse River. He hired a few black men from Canada to help him through his haying and harvesting and with other odd jobs around the Nowlin homestead. Two of the men kept their names to themselves, and the names of two of the other men were Campbell and Obadiah. According to William Nowlin, Campbell was the older of the two and trusty and dependable in all respects. Obadiah was a young man whose parents had died when he was a child. He had a younger sister and brother, and he wanted to keep them together and provide a home for them. The young woman kept house for Nowlin's three workmen, and she frequently came down to his house and helped his wife.

The Fugitive Slave Law required northern men to help hunt down and capture runaway slaves, so William did not inquire too closely into the histories of the men who worked for him. Campbell told William Nowlin the details of his escape from slavery, and William realized that the men were afraid that they would be arrested and taken back into slavery. They didn't feel safe in working so far from Canada, but Nowlin's attitude should have reassured them. He said, "I am sure if I had heard of his master's approach, or his agent's, I should have conducted him, or the three, six miles, through the woods to Detroit River, procured a boat and sent them across to Canada, regretting the existence of 'the Fugitive Slave Law' and obeying a higher law."

After William Nowlin had finished his haying and harvesting, the black workers moved back to Canada near Windsor, illustrating a phenomenon that historians often overlook—the fluidity of the border between Detroit and Windsor and how often freedmen, slaves and white families crossed and recrossed it.

Halmor Emmons was another early settler on the Ecorse River. Born in 1814 at Sandy Hill, a small town in upstate New York, Halmor dedicated to books the long hours that other boys his age spent playing sports. He completed his law studies, and in 1836 he moved to Detroit and established himself as a lawyer. The long hours of practicing law impaired his health, and at one point it appeared that he would develop tuberculosis. A friend suggested that Emmons move east to what is now Grosse Pointe, and another friend advised him to experience the bracing air of the Upper Peninsula. Emmons decided to experiment. He consulted a medicine man of the Wyandotte Indians, who directed him to the point of the Ecorse River that was located just over the border in Wyandotte. This area contained mineral deposits, and the Indians looked on it as a healing ground. Emmons invested in an estate of 622 acres. He planted orchards and young pear and apple trees, which remain to this day, surrounding his home near the riverbank. In summer, always in sight of the riverbank, the music of the bullfrogs lulled him to sleep. The waterways were the main way to travel in those early days, and the Ecorse River was an important water route since it flowed in several branches at least fifty miles inland and connected to the Detroit River in several spots.

Another early resident, Dr. George B. Russel, learned about the Ecorse River on horseback. Born in 1815, Russel was a circuit-riding doctor. For twenty-seven years, from about 1842 to 1869, he rode his circuit, taking in both sides of the Detroit River from Trenton to the bay fifteen miles above Detroit and, on the Canadian side, from Malden to Belle River, eighteen

The Tank family and others rowed across Ecorse Creek and camped on Emmons Boulevard in the early decades of the twentieth century.

Camping on Ecorse Creek included enjoying gentle breezes and good food.

miles above Windsor, as well as the Gratiot road to Mount Clemens and Romeo, Woodward Avenue to Pontiac, Grand River Road to Farmington and Michigan Avenue to Dearborn and Wayne.

Dr. Russel heard that a camp of Indians at Conners Creek had contracted smallpox, and after he arrived at the camp and examined the Indians, he discovered the disease in six or eight lodges. Richard Connor and his sister, Therese, helped Dr. Russel vaccinate seven hundred Indians in twenty-four hours, and not one of the exposed Indians died.

The Campau family is also intimately connected with the history of Ecorse. Alexander Campau was born on September 7, 1843, back in the days when Indians still inhabited Ecorse and its neighboring lands and when the stagecoach was making its first run between Detroit and Monroe. The second child and oldest son of Mr. and Mrs. Alexis Campau, he came into the world in a small frame house with hand-nailed walls located on Jefferson Avenue in Ecorse.

As a child he attended a little frame schoolhouse on Salliotte Road with a handful of other boys gathered to learn the three "Rs" with the guidance of one long-suffering teacher. His father died when he was just eight years old, and Alexander helped his mother in the fields and in the house, as well. To make ends meet, Mrs. Campau rented rooms in her house to men who had come to the area to work on the area's first railroad, the Lakeshore Railroad. One of her boarders working on the railroad was a stalwart Indian who took an instant liking to Alex. The Indian and Alex shared a bed for most of the time that he boarded at the Campau home, and Alex learned firsthand the "true, friendly nature" of the Indians living around Ecorse.

Alex also enjoyed the boyhood adventure of riding from Detroit to Monroe and back on the stagecoach, which was driven by a distant cousin of his. He loved pulling into Monroe at night, hot, dusty and weary, and listening to the travelers spinning tall tales as he ate supper. The next day, rising at dawn to catch the stage home, he felt a renewed sense of adventure as he headed to Ecorse along the River Road. As he grew older, Alex worked with his brother and took his threshing machine to neighboring farmers who had none. He truck farmed for himself and sold his produce to neighbors and to people around the area. When the Tecumseh Salt Works was founded in Ecorse, Alex was one of its first employees, helping to clear away the marshlands.

On July 24, 1866, when he was twenty-three years old, Alex hitched up his horse and buggy and picked up Adis Salliotte, who lived a half mile away from the Campaus. They drove all the way to Wyandotte and were married. Returning to Ecorse, they worked together on Alex's farm. The Campaus had five children, and Adis died in 1923. Lillian and Agnes never married, and Alex lived with them in his old age. Florence married into the Drouillard family, but they lived close to Alex. His son, Ernest, lived near him, and another son died in infancy. Alex died on August 24, 1940, and was buried in Ecorse Cemetery.

Moses Salliotte's farm was situated on the land now known as Salliotte Road up to Bonzano (now known as Outer Drive). This former farmland is bordered now by the series of railroad tracks directly to the west and by Jefferson Avenue directly to the east. Moses Salliotte built a log cabin with an earthen floor at the site of present-day Loveland's Drugstore. Then he built a log cabin near Ecorse Creek, and his son, Oliver, and grandson, Eli, were born in the cabin. Moses died on the old homestead when his grandson Eli was four or five years old. Antoine Salliotte bought a six-hundred-acre farm directly from France and located to the east of the farm that Moses owned. He built a house large enough to accommodate his growing family and serve as a place for funerals, weddings and parties.

Salliotte family tradition has it that Alexis Saliot built the first log cabin on the shore of the Detroit River near the mouth of the Riviere aux Ecorses, now Ecorse Creek. Family tradition also says that the earliest members of the family came to North America from the Alsace-Lorraine section of France with the early Jesuits and made their way to Michigan with the pioneer priest-explorer Father Pierre Marquette. One of the earliest mentions of the Saliot name in Michigan occurs in a census of Detroit taken in 1779. Jean Saliot and his wife and two children are listed. Jean Saliot married

Marie Magdalene Jourdain, and they had two sons, Jean Baptiste and Alexis Moses Salliotte, and two daughters, Marie (who married Joseph Bondie) and Therese (who married Dominique Bondie). Jean Baptiste Salliotte married Marie Jeanne Bondie in Detroit in 1799, and after she died in 1816, he married Catherine Chene, who died in 1822. He was the only member of the family listed in the 1820 census of Detroit.

Evidently, Alexis Moses Salliotte was the first representative of his family in the Down River area. He and his wife, Archange Bourassa, had two sons, Moses and Hyacinth. Moses Salliotte was born in Ecorse in 1807, according to his tombstone in the Ecorse Cemetery, and he married Charlotte Cook, born in Yorkshire, England, in 1815. Old-time residents of Ecorse, talking to Moses Salliotte before he died in 1892, recalled that he spoke little English. His wife Charlotte taught him a few words of English after their marriage, but he mostly spoke French.

Moses and Charlotte had five children, including Alexis M., Joseph, Gilbert, Julian, Florence (who married Joseph Drouillard) and Anne (1845–1930), who married her cousin, Oliver Salliotte. Alexis M. Salliotte was born in 1837 and married Mary Sylvia Rousson. He became an active political figure in the Down River area and served many years as treasurer and clerk of Ecorse Township. He was postmaster of Ecorse for nearly twenty years, and when Ecorse was incorporated as a village in 1902, he was elected first village president.

The children of Alexis and Mary included Cora Lefebre, Frances Monahan, Alma O'Boyle, Etta Nelson, Elizabeth Graffan, Eleanor and Adan Salliotte and Simon, who married Louise Loeffler but had no children. Joseph Salliotte, second son of Moses and Charlotte, was Ecorse village assessor from 1903 to 1906. He married Marie Rouleau and, after Marie died, Mary Moran. His children included Emma Labadie, Charlotte Adan, Gertrude Cummins and the late Ignatius J. Salliotte, prominent Down River lawyer, who served as a member of the state constitutional convention in 1907 and was Lincoln Park's first village attorney.

Gilbert Salliotte, third son of Moses, never married. He enlisted in the army during the Civil War and was shot through the cheek and mouth. Hyacinth Salliotte, brother of Moses and second son of the pioneer Alexis, was born in 1810 and married Adelaide Labadie. Their children included Mary; Samuel, a Civil War veteran; Cleophus, who married Juliette Labadie; Antoine, who married Agnes Abbott; Adis, who married Alex Campau; Angelique; and Peter.

Antoine, born in 1841, was also a Civil War veteran and served with Company H., Fourteenth Michigan Infantry. He marched through Georgia with General William T. Sherman and was twice wounded in action. He is buried in Ecorse Cemetery. Antoine's children include Ecorse municipal judge Alger E. Salliotte, who held his judicial post from 1934 to the 1950s, and Roy B. Salliotte, who was killed at the Battle of the Meuse-Argonne in France in 1918. The Roy B. Salliotte American Legion Post in Ecorse was named for him.

CHAPTER 3

ECORSE COMMERCE
COMMENCES

The French settlers built pirogues and bateaux to use on the Detroit River and its tributaries, including the Ecorse River. The pirogue was a large wooden canoe made from hollowing a tree and splitting it lengthwise, using the halves for the sides of a boat made from planking in the bottom and ends. These pirogues could carry three tons of freight and crews of six who paddled and poled the craft close to shore and beached it easily. A bateaux was an open flat-bottomed boat built of cut timber that could be as big as a barge—at least sixty feet long, carrying fifteen tons of cargo and a crew of twelve. In deep water, the crew moved the bateaux with oars. In shallow water, they poled it or towed it from the shore.

Settlers along the Ecorse River also used birch-bark canoes and, later in the century, rowboats. An early *Detroit Free Press* advertisement attests to the commercial value of both land and bateaux:

> *Bateau For Sale*
> *The subscriber offers for sale a new land and well made Batteau. She has a deck in her stem and will carry between sixty and seventy Barrels. She will be sold at a reasonable price for cash down, or, a credit will be given on good security. For further particulars apply to*
> *GEORGE CAMPBELL*
> *River aux Ecorse, June 16, 1820*

In 1827, the Michigan territorial legislature reorganized Wayne County, which since 1796 had comprised the major portion of the Lower Peninsula of Michigan, forming Ecorse and several other townships. The United States Congressional Ordinance of 1787 had established the Northwest Territory and set forth land policies for the recognition of old French land grants.

As a result, Ecorse Township at its creation consisted of fifty-four square miles and comprised several old private claims, more than forty sections and partial sections of land and two small islands in the Detroit River.

The first township meeting took place in the home of Daniel Goodell, and John Cicotte was named supervisor. His duties included protecting the public health, speaking for the township and arbitrating all disputes. At this point, Ecorse Township included the territory that later became Taylor Township in 1848.

Simon Rousseau, A. Labadie, L. Bourassa and P. LeBlanc made the first plot of the village in 1836 and named it Grandport. Grandport was a small hamlet only four blocks long and stood where present-day Southfield and Jefferson Avenue meet. A fishing and farming center, it was the only settlement between Detroit and Monroe for many years. An 1829 map in the Burton Historical Museum in Detroit reveals that Grandport streets were named after Revolutionary War heroes—Jefferson, Monroe, Webster and Jackson—and also after the French settlers St. Cosme, Labadie and LeBlanc. The village of Grandport had eight hundred people, 152 homes and four businesses. It became the hub of the neighboring farmlands and the site of a shipyard, as well as Raupp's Lumber Mill. Ecorse was platted as the small, unincorporated village of Grandport in 1834 and was incorporated as a village in 1903. It became a city in 1942 in a final break from the township. When Ecorse was incorporated as a city, the township seat was moved for the first time to the then village of Allen Park. It remained there until 1956 when Allen Park's imminent incorporation prompted its removal to the unincorporated area of the township.

Eventually people began to call the village of Grandport Ecorse, even though a map drawn about 1830 still shows the village of Grandport. Streets that exist presently in their original locations are High, Labadie, Bourassa and White. What was then State Street is now Southfield Road, and Lafforter Street has been renamed LeBlanc. Grandport was the center of Ecorse Township but was never incorporated, and eventually the name fell into disuse. Most of the old-timers called their community Ecorse.

Along with Ecorse, old French pioneer families like the Goodells, Monties, Campaus and Cicottes were changing from a farming to commercial focus, and hints of industrial growth hummed in the air. Industry and technology were beginning to transform the Down River area from a stretch of sleepy riverside communities to a humming industrial shore. Judge H.H. Emmons lived in Ecorse then, as did the Salliotte and Cicotte families. Alexander Bondie ran a saloon on the northeast corner of State and Jefferson. Campau and Ferguson had a grocery business on the corner of State and Monroe,

Ecorse Commerce Commences

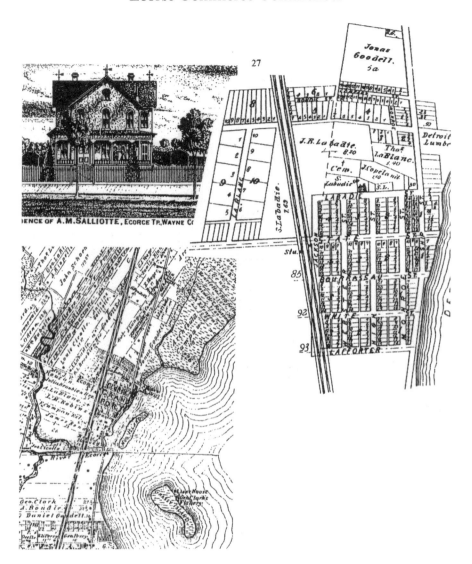

In 1836, Alexis Labadie, Simeon Rousseau, L. Bourassa and P. White platted and recorded a four-block-long settlement called Grandport. It was located near Southfield and West Jefferson.

and John Copeland ran a lumber company, Frederick Ferguson, a brickyard. G.R. Goodell operated a grocery store, and E.J. Goodell had a feed store on the east side of Jefferson, just north of Southfield. J.B. Montie oversaw his blacksmith shop south of the Detroit, Toledo & Ironton Railroad, and George Cicotte owned a general store on Bourassa and West Jefferson and A.M. Salliotte on Jefferson and State Street.

Wyandotte Rolling Mills was doing quite well in 1873. The *Detroit Evening News* noted that the Wyandotte Rolling Mills was to manufacture one thousand tons of rails for the Burlington & Southwestern Railroad. Also, Wyandotte Rolling Mills had specimens of iron for exhibition at the state fair, which withstood tests averaging 25 percent over government tests.

By 1873, the business directory listed fifteen establishments in Ecorse:

Alexander Bondie, Saloon	*Corner State and Jefferson, N.E.*
Campau and Ferguson, Grocers	*SW Corner of State and Monroe*
Louis Cicotte, Hotel Proprietor	*Jefferson, across from C.F. Smith*
John Copeland, Lumber Manufacturer	*Site covered by oil tanks*
Detroit River Lumber Company Sawmill	*Beaubin Slip*
Judge H.H. Emmons, U.S. District Court	*40 feet back on Jefferson*
Frederick Ferguson, Brick Layer	*Corner Southfield and Monroe Streets*
G.R. Goodell, Grocer	*Across from Liggetts*
E.J. Goodell	*Surveyor & Feed Store—East Side of Jefferson, just north of Southfield*
N.L. LeBlanc & Riopelle, grocers	
J.B. Montie, blacksmith	*South of Detroit, Toledo & Ironton Railroad*
Louis Odion, shoemaker	*Monroe Street between Southfield & Bourassa*
Michael Roulo, Hotel Proprietor	
A.M. Salliotte, General Store and Notary Public	*Jefferson and State Street*
Joseph Salliotte, butcher	*Old Fish Market*

There were a few small mills and lumberyards along Ecorse Creek, and Raupp's Lumber Mill began to operate on Jefferson Avenue, where the Ecorse Creek joined the Detroit River. Fishing on a small commercial scale employed some men, and fishing and trapping helped supplement farm incomes, but Ecorse still didn't enjoy large manufacturing growth. In 1880, Richard Beaubien of Detroit had six large icehouses built in Ecorse, which furnished work to men who had but little.

Alexis M. Salliotte and Gustave Raupp joined forces in the 1880s to run the Salliotte & Raupp mill at a profit. The mill was strategically located on the banks

Ecorse Commerce Commences

Men worked the saws continuously at Salliotte and Raupp's Mill to fashion pine logs into finished lumber. They also deposited gigantic piles of sawdust and wood shavings along the banks of Ecorse Creek.

of Ecorse Creek. From after the Civil War until about the 1880s, Michigan enjoyed a timber boom, supplying almost all of the lumber used in the United States. After lumberjacks cut down the trees, they were loaded on huge log rafts that were towed down Lake Huron from Alpena and Bay City into the Detroit River and up Ecorse Creek to Salliotte & Raupp's sawmill. Men worked the saws continuously to fashion the pine logs into finished lumber. This gigantic lumber production resulted in equally gigantic piles of sawdust and wood shavings along the banks of Ecorse Creek. Veteran employees of the Evans Motor Sales Auto Dealership that occupied a salesroom on Jefferson recalled that the dealership had been built over mounds of sawdust from the mill.

After the lumber was sawed and smoothed into logs, it was loaded onto boats and shipped to Detroit, and in Detroit the lumber was loaded onto railroad freight cars and sent to communities all across the country. If the timber was consigned to local communities, it was loaded into wagons pulled by teams of horses and oxen and hauled out onto Mill Road and into present-day Lincoln Park, Southgate, Allen Park and Taylor, to be used in constructing homes and businesses. The old Mill Road came to be called Mill Street because of these lumber days and not because of the Michigan Steel Corporation, which wasn't built on Mill Street until 1924.

Gustave Raupp was not a wealthy man when he moved to Ecorse from Germany, but he was far-sighted and ambitious enough to establish a sawmill on the banks of Ecorse Creek during the Michigan timber boom. He was also astute enough to enter a partnership with Alexis M. Salliotte. In today's dollars, Alexis Salliotte would be a millionaire, and by 1870s standards he was a wealthy man. He owned extensive timber stands near Ashley, Michigan, and took full capitalistic advantage of the lumber boom. When the boom ended in the late 1880s, Salliotte and Raupp dissolved their partnership, but Gustave Raupp continued to operate the mill. After he died in 1923, his sons ran the business for several years. Then in 1929, a spectacular fire that burned out of control for nearly twenty-four hours destroyed the mill.

Besides the houses that were built with their timber, street names in Ecorse and Lincoln Park are visible survivors of Salliotte's and Raupp's legacies. For many years, the home of Alexis Salliotte with its round-towered rooms, cupola and Victorian gingerbread stood as an Ecorse landmark on the corner of Southfield and High Streets, but it was torn down in the 1970s and replaced with an apartment complex. Two Ecorse streets—Alexis and Salliotte—were named in memory of Alexis Salliotte, who also served as the first village president of Ecorse when it was incorporated in 1902. There is a Raupp Street in Lincoln Park, and Gustave Raupp is also remembered as a founding member of the Ecorse Boat Club. Mill Street, which runs through Ecorse, crosses River Drive and continues into Lincoln Park, is a reminder of the days when horses pulling heavy wagonloads of wood for houses plodded down its length heading to new home and business sites.

CHAPTER 4

ECORSE AND THE
UNDERGROUND RAILROAD

C ensus documents from the eighteenth and nineteenth centuries record varying numbers of slaves in Detroit and up and down the Detroit River but firmly establish their existence. A 1762 census for Detroit reveals that 65 of the approximately 900 people living near the fort were African American slaves. Governor Henry Hamilton listed 78 female slaves and 79 male slaves in a later census. By July 1832, approximately 300 Negroes lived in and outside of Detroit, many of them runaway slaves. Most of them had found work, so they remained in Detroit instead of crossing into Canada and assured freedom. Many of them moved back and forth across the border as laws and the determination of slave catchers waxed and waned and opportunities for a better living and greater safety for themselves and their families fluctuated between Canada and the United States.

It is as difficult to document the tracks of the Underground Railroad in Ecorse as it is to follow them across the country because of the necessary secrecy surrounding its operations. Detroit, however, was a major Underground Railroad station, and Down River communities like Ecorse were involved because of proximity, as well as abolitionism. The fact that the Detroit River flowing through the Down River communities is studded with islands like Bois Blanc, Grassy and Fighting Island that served as rest stops for fugitive slaves and their pursuers made Ecorse a magnet for fugitive slaves. Before and during the Civil War, escaping slaves used Bois Blanc or Bo-Lo Island as a station stop on the Underground Railroad route to Canada. They landed on the beach and rested for a few hours or a few days before continuing on to Amherstburg and new lives in Canada. Local tradition has it that fugitive slaves also used Fighting Island and Grassy Island as stepping stones to Canada.

Captains of Great Lakes vessels used sextants, compasses, the Big Dipper and the North Star as navigational guides and their moral compasses to determine whether to transport fugitive slaves. With the help of Great Lakes captains or in small skiffs, canoes, rowboats or anything that floated, fugitive slaves crossed the river to freedom. "Old man" is a slang term for a captain, and many of the "old men" of the Great Lakes vessels were abolitionists and carried fugitive slaves to freedom. A smaller number worked to keep or return the fugitives to captivity.

Free African Canadians and fugitive slaves from America quarried stone near the town of Amherstburg, Ontario. Black-owned vessels then shipped the stone blocks up the Detroit River to the port of Detroit, where they were loaded onto another ship and carried to the site of the first Sault Ste. Marie Canal that opened in 1855. This canal allowed ships to move freely from one lake to another and began the transporting of Lake Superior iron ore to the Midwest.

Black and white crewmen helped escaping slaves cross the lakes to freedom in Canada. George DeBaptiste of Detroit was one of the active conductors in the nautical Underground Railroad. Purchasing the steamboat *T. Whitney* in 1860, he ran it between various Canadian ports and Detroit and later forged a direct link across Lake Erie between the ports of Sandusky, Ohio and Detroit. He made wood stops at the port of Amherstburg, Ontario. After the *T. Whitney* renewed its wood supply, it steamed out to the Detroit River, and any fugitive slaves that happened to be onboard were left at the dock to begin their lives in Canada.

The *Pearl*, a steamer plying between Amherstburg, Ontario and Detroit, played an important part in the lives of many fugitive slaves, including John Freeman Walls and his white wife and her white children. Captain Christopher C. Allen, a native of Amherstburg, sailed the *Pearl* as a wheelsman and a porter between 1859 and 1863 and piloted many runaway slaves on the Detroit docks to freedom.

"The Ward Line," a ballad from the traditional Great Lakes music collection at the Bentley Historical Library in Ann Arbor, Michigan, addresses the reality of black sailors. Copper and iron ore were shipped from Michigan's Upper Peninsula and other Lake Superior ports on wooden hulled ships that were loaded by wheelbarrow. This was a backbreaking job, and freed slaves were used as laborers in Samuel Ward's shipping company. They enjoyed a "free ride" while the ship sailed, but in port they worked nonstop until the cargo was unloaded.

The Ward line of ships and its crews generally sympathized with fugitive slaves and carried them to Canada. Fittingly enough, Captain Eber B. Ward's story begins in Canada, where he was born in 1811. His parents had fled to Canada from Vermont in 1811 to avoid the consequences of the War of 1812, so Eber was born an American citizen. After moving around for several years, the Ward family finally settled in Marine City, Michigan. From the time he could dog paddle, Eber Ward longed to sail on the lakes, and luckily for him, his Uncle Samuel, the leading shipbuilder of Marine City, noticed and tapped his enthusiasm for Great Lakes shipping. Eber and Samuel Ward built and operated many vessels that traversed the Great Lakes and deposited fugitive slaves in Canada. Their vessels included the *General Harrison*, the *Huron*, the *Detroit*, the *Samuel Ward*, the *Atlantic*, the *Ocean*, the *Arctic*, the *Pearl*, the *B.F. Wade*, the *Planet* and the *Montgomery*.

Free black sailors and escaped slaves worked on Great Lakes ships and helped many fugitive slaves gain their freedom, and white vessel captains risked losing their ships to help runaway slaves, especially after the passage of the Fugitive Slave Law of 1850. General Reed's boats stopping at Racine, Wisconsin, took fugitives without charging them a fare. The general owned five boats: the *Sultana*, the *James Madison*, the *Missouri*, the *Niagara* and the *Keystone State*. The *Sultana* was an eight-hundred-ton steamer built at Trenton, Michigan, in 1847. Before it wrecked in 1858, the *Sultana* transported many fugitive slaves under the command of Captain Gil Appleby, who died in Buffalo in 1867.

The *James Madison*, built in Erie, Pennsylvania, in 1837, and the *Missouri*, built in Erie in 1840, carried fugitive slaves to freedom in Canada, and so did the steamer *Niagara*. The *Chicago Express* of April 11, 1844, carried news of the *Missouri*: "Arrived here this morning from Buffalo, which place she left on Thursday last. The *Missouri* is the first steamer from below which has entered our port this season."

The *Keystone State*, a 1,354-ton steamer built at Buffalo, New York, in 1849, also transported runaway slaves to freedom. One of its captains was W.P. Stone, favorably known on the Great Lakes. The steamer *Illinois*, captained by Chelsea Blake and running between Chicago and Detroit, was also a safe ship for passengers going to Canada.

Captain Steele of the propeller *Galena* helped fugitive slaves, and so did Captain Kelsey of the *Chesapeake*. John G. Weiblen navigated the Great Lakes in 1855 and 1856 and transported many fugitives from Chicago to Collingwood, Ontario.

The *Forest Queen*, the *Morning Star* and the *May Queen* running between Cleveland and Detroit carried many slaves to freedom. The steamer *Mayflower*, built by the Michigan Central Railroad Company, was the finest steamer on the lakes in its day. Its crew actively participated in the transfer of fugitive slaves to Canada.

Ecorse had two active American Legion posts—Great Lakes Steel American Legion Post 272 and Roy B. Salliotte Post No. 319. The Salliotte Post was chartered in 1933.

The Ecorse World War II monument at the Detroit riverfront features the names of hundreds of Ecorse World War II veterans. Ecorse has contributed soldiers to every war in which the United States participated.

Ecorse and the Underground Railroad

Lake Erie, and its many port cities, provided one of the quickest and most friendly routes to Canada, particularly Buffalo and Detroit, because only the narrow Niagara and Detroit Rivers separated fugitives from freedom in Canada. Newspapers miles and states away often reported on fugitive slave traffic in Detroit. In 1859, a small-town Wisconsin newspaper, the *Oconomowoc Free Press*, reported that during the week of December 8, 1859, the Underground Railroad had brought twenty-six Negroes to Detroit.

Ecorse soldiers and citizens on land also actively participated in the Underground Railroad and fought in the Civil War. At least two black soldiers from Ecorse, Thomas Seymore, age twenty-three, and Samuel Pearee, age nineteen, fought in the First Michigan Colored Infantry.

The Fourteenth Michigan Infantry, Company H, contributed at least fifteen Ecorse soldiers to the Civil War, including Alexander Bondy, Francis Labot, Joseph Laduke, Pascoh Odette, Peter Rabindeau, Antoine Salliotte, John Short and Samuel Smith. Pascoh Odette was killed on the outskirts of Atlanta on August 7, 1864.

Louis Beaubien and Anthony Reno, both from the Twenty-fourth Michigan Infantry, are buried in Ecorse Cemetery. George and Joachim Theek of Ecorse were both from the First Michigan Light Artillery.

Ecorse Civil War soldiers buried in Ecorse Cemetery include Louis Beabien, John Brest, Charles Cicotte, Oliver Delisle, Gregory Drouillard, Solomon Drouillard, Elijah J. Goodell, Gabriel Goodell, Peter Jager, Louis Montry, Antoine Salliotte, Gilbert Salliotte, Thomas H. Somers and William Young. Antoine Salliott served with General Sherman in his famous march through Georgia and was twice wounded in action.

CHAPTER 5

ECORSE GOES TO SCHOOL
AND CHURCH

E corse developed its own cultural institutions at its own pace. The earliest
school records aren't available, but it is probable that more French than
English was spoken in the first schools established. In most cases, the French
culture and customs predominated, even in homes where one partner was
English or some other nationality. Older Ecorse residents recall being told
of a log school, located near the shore of the river at the foot of what is now
Labadie Street. Some also recall a small building on the corner of Jefferson
and White that served as a school in the 1860s. Later, classes were held
in the band building and in the council chambers of the old city hall. By
the 1930s, Ecorse had built a high school and three grade schools, and St.
Francis Elementary and High School had been already been operating for
a few years.

St. Francis Xavier Catholic Church became a parish in 1845 and served
the communities of Fort Wayne, River Rouge, Wyandotte, Oakwood and
Delray. Families intermarried, and eventually there were nearly equal
numbers of French and English settlers. The first recorded mixed marriage
was that of James Goodell and Angelique Salliotte. At that time, Ecorse had
only a small mission where Father Gabriel Richard preached once a month,
but this Ecorse mission became the nucleus of the present St. Francis Xavier
Parish. Father Gabriel Richard was the most influential pioneer priest, and
he established Ecorse connections, as well. He founded St. Francis Xavier
Church in Ecorse as a mission of Saint Anne's Church, Detroit, for the
pioneer Catholics of the Down River area. The only Catholic priest in
Michigan territory from 1806 until 1821, Father Richard served about five
hundred families spread out along the eastern shores of the Detroit River,
Lake St. Clair and Lake Huron from Ecorse to Port Huron. Father Richard
often came by water to Ecorse to say Mass at the Pierre LeBlanc log house

Mayor Dick Manning (center) and the Headstart staff and children.

Ecorse High School of the 1950s and 1960s consisted of old and new parts. One new part featured Miss Jessman's greenhouse jutting out onto the lawn.

Ecorse Goes to School and Church

The original 1929 Ecorse High School had classrooms that smelled strongly of chalk, including room 212, the home of Miss Elliott.

on Jefferson Avenue. It served as a place of worship for early Catholics, and for many years Mass was said within its primitive walls.

Father Richard took a census in 1808 and in 1832. After finishing a long missionary journey around Michigan, he reported 926 families averaging 6 persons and "150 Catholic Irishmen scattered here and there." They were part of the passenger list of the *Walk-in-the-Water*, the first steamboat on the Great Lakes that made the voyage from Buffalo to Detroit in 1818.

The first St. Francis Xavier Church was built on High Street and Bourassa and dedicated in 1882. Father Charles DePreitre, the first resident pastor of St. Francis Xavier, was a nephew of Bishop Lefevre, who had come to Detroit as a seminarian and was ordained there on May 31, 1848. Father DePreitre served as pastor of St. Francis Xavier until 1870 and also acted as mission priest of parishes in Wyandotte and Trenton in Wayne County and Newport in Monroe County. Father Louis Baroux became St. Francis Xavier pastor in 1871 and remained there until 1882.

Father John Van Gennip served as first pastor of the pioneer church, and the parish record states that on May 20, 1882, Reverend J.T. Van Gennip blessed a cemetery known as Ecorse Cemetery with a potter's field in the northeast corner. His tombstone is located in the cemetery that he founded,

The old St. Francis Church stood on High and Bourassa Streets, and its cornerstone was laid in 1882. Father J. Van Gennip served as pastor.

and it simply notes that he was the pastor of St. Francis Xavier Church, born in Heeze, Holland, on July 2, 1818, and died in Ecorse on September 3, 1889.

Even though the cemetery wasn't blessed until 1882, church records indicate that the first burial in St. Francis Xavier Cemetery took place in 1848 when Charlotte Cook, wife of Moses Salliotte, was laid to rest on

Ecorse Goes to School and Church

His Eminence Edward Cardinal Mooney blessed the portals of the New St. Francis Xavier Church as part of the dedication ceremony in December 1953.

September 7. Only thirty-three years old when she died, Charlotte was born in Yorkshire, England. Moses Salliotte also rests nearby. His epitaph reveals that he died on March 9, 1892, at the age of eighty-five. He was born in Ecorse and was one of the earliest settlers in the village.

A visit to the old St. Francis Cemetery or Ecorse Cemetery on Third Street is a trip through history, with old names and dates on every headstone. Although Father Richard is not buried in the cemetery of his mission church, ironically the descendants of Francois Labadie repose there. The Labadie family is one of the founding families of Ecorse, and Charles, Henry, John, Alexander, Elizabeth, Florence and Michael are just are few of the Labadies resting in the cemetery.

Ecorse Protestants expanded in the shadow of Father Richard's mission church. Tradition has it that there was a Protestant Sunday school in Ecorse as early as the 1870s. Some of the Ecorse citizens of the 1870s most certainly participated in the Sunday schools. Most likely these early Sunday schools were held in private homes just as the early Catholic Masses were held in the Goodell log cabin. Jefferson Avenue was a dirt road that turned into thick, clingy mud when it rained and icy ruts that rattled buggy wheels and clenched teeth in the winter, and people weren't too inclined to seek an out-of-town Sunday school.

By 1907, a streetcar ran through Trenton, Wyandotte, River Rouge and Ecorse, making it easier for people to travel, although Jefferson Avenue was still unpaved and turned just as muddy and rutted in the corresponding seasons. Despite, or maybe because of, travel hardships between Ecorse and Wyandotte, a group of young people who were members of the Wyandotte Baptist Church but lived in Ecorse wanted to have a local church service to attend. On September 1, 1907, they organized a mission Sunday school in Ecorse, and on September 12, 1910, the Ecorse Presbyterian Church was organized and chartered by the Presbytery of Detroit with fifty-one charter members including Miss Ida Stevenson, Arthur Schultz, Henry W. Gerlach and Frank Seavitte. The newly organized church members met in a wooden frame building on the corner of Monroe and Cicotte Streets, but in 1912 a wind storm blew it down. Presbyterians and townspeople immediately rallied to build a new church. They selected a lot on the corner of Outer Drive and Jefferson Avenue, and several people donated their teams of horses to dig out the basement of the church. By 1914, a new brick church stood sentinel over Ecorse from that corner and remained there for the next fifty-six years.

Reverend Roy G. Hershey became the first pastor of the Ecorse Presbyterian Church on December 15, 1910, and guided the church into its new brick building. Ecorse pioneer Eli "Peck" LeBlanc remembered that Reverend Hershey was a handsome young bachelor, which helped him sell bricks for the new church. According to Peck, even several people from St. Francis Xavier bought Presbyterian bricks from Reverend Hershey because he was such a persuasive preacher.

While Isaac J. Van Hee served as pastor from 1913 to 1914, Ecorse retained its small pastoral village character. In fact, it had just become a village in 1903, with Alexis M. Salliotte as its first village president. The *Detroit Free Press* described the Ecorse of Reverend Van Hee and Reverend David Gilles (1914–15) as "the Little Venice of the West End" because so many cottages were perched on the end of piers jutting out into the Detroit River to get the full advantage of the river breezes. Farms still outnumbered industries, and the few industries that existed were based on natural resources, such as lumber and shipyards.

By the time the Reverends C.W. Hastings (1917–21), Walter Nichol (1921–26) and William T. Angus (1926–28) had come and gone as pastors of the Presbyterian Church, Ecorse had grown a modern face. The 2.5-square-mile village had attracted George Fink, who established the Michigan Steel Corporation and expanded it into Great Lakes Steel Corporation. Great Lakes Engineering and Nicholson Terminal Dock Company expanded an already well-established maritime tradition in Ecorse via building, repairing

Built in 1899 at the corner of High and Labadie Streets, the old Ecorse Village Hall stood until 1948 as one of the Down River area's oldest landmarks.

and docking ships. The Presbyterian manse next to the church was also built in 1926 when Reverend Angus was pastor of the church.

At this point in its history, Ecorse had five schools: School One at High and Labadie, School Two on West Josephine, School Three on Sixth and White Streets, Ecorse High School on Seventh and Bonzano and St. Francis Elementary and High School. Besides the Presbyterian Church, St. Francis Xavier Catholic Church, the Salvation Army, the Gospel Tabernacle, the Church of God, the First Baptist and Mount Zion Baptist were among the Ecorse churches that ministered to the spiritual needs of the village. The main library, the Municipal Building and Visger Road branches provided books for Ecorse citizens, and the city hall at High and Labadie had meeting rooms for spelling bees and community events.

Reverend Leonard Duckett and his family came to Ecorse in 1931, and over the next twenty-five years, he contributed much toward the betterment of his church and the community. He provided a strong, steady pastoral influence to the Ecorse Presbyterian Church. He oversaw its expansion and remodeling to coincide with the widening of Jefferson Avenue in 1937. While the Presbyterian Church was being remodeled, the congregation met for a time in Raupp's Hall, and Reverend Duckett revealed his sense of humor when he commented wryly that the remnants of pumpkins

45

In the late 1940s, Ecorse mayor William Voisine helped to build a new library on the corner of Outer Drive and West Jefferson.

and other decorations from a Halloween party the night before "took him aback." As well as serving his church, Reverend Duckett served his community, including several years as a member of the library board.

The Presbyterians were building again in 1953, this time a new youth center adjacent to the manse and church. Reverend Duckett helped the Church House Youth Center become a reality, and after he retired in 1956, the building was renamed the Leonard Duckett Center. Many events of the church and community have taken place at the Leonard Duckett Center over the years, including Sunday school, Youth Fellowship, Kiwanis Club, Rotary, Civil Air Cadets, Boy Scouts, Alcoholics Anonymous, Narcotics Anonymous, Ecorse Women's Club, Square Dancers, Women's Fellowship Association, rummage sales, Women's Bible Class, study groups, fish fry suppers, spaghetti dinners, Harvest Home Suppers and bazaars.

During the twenty-five years that Reverend Duckett served in Ecorse, the village went though several changes. It survived a lawless rumrunning era in the late 1920s and early 1930s, when shots could be heard daily and nightly, bodies could often be spotted floating in the river and a Wild West–style

The Women's Fellowship Group of the Ecorse Presbyterian Church cooked thousands of delicious dinners over the nearly one-hundred-year history of the church.

gunfight between citizens and rumrunners took place in Hogan's Alley off Jefferson Avenue. These were Depression years, and Reverend Duckett helped his parishioners meet the challenges of putting food on the table daily and keeping a roof over their heads. He also addressed the problem of paying the church mortgage and successfully kept the church roof and ownership in the hands of the Presbyterians.

After Reverend Leonard Duckett retired in 1956, the Detroit Presbytery and the National Office of the Presbyterian Church sponsored a Detroit Industrial Ministry, with the Ecorse Presbyterian Church as the focal point of the experiment. Three young ministers, all recent graduates of Princeton Theological Seminary, came to lead the vocational ministry to the men in the large industrial plants of Ecorse. Reverend Orion C. Hopper and Reverend David B. Lowry served from 1956 to 1958, and Reverend George Coleman remained as pastor until 1962. Ecorse Presbyterian Church grew in numbers—with peak membership of four hundred people—and influence during this experiment.

Ecorse is a city of churches, including the Faith Christian Assembly, with members shown here.

Grove Baptist Church celebrates its anniversary. The Episcopal Church of the Resurrection in Ecorse also celebrated its tenth anniversary in Ecorse in March 1958.

Ecorse Goes to School and Church

The First Missionary Baptist Church has been located in Ecorse since 1922. It was formerly known as Lily of the Valley Church.

Reverend John Pack served the church from 1963 to 1964, and in 1965 Reverend Raymond Dana Scott and his family came to the Ecorse Presbyterian Church. During the 1965–71 ministry of Reverend Scott, he and the congregation met the challenge of replacing the old church building, which engineers advised them would cost more to repair than replace. The new church was dedicated on February 22, 1970, and in the dedication program Reverend Scott summed up his feelings about the new building when he wrote: "There are many other things that one could say about the symbolism and theology of this building but unless this building truly becomes a means for fulfilling the mission of God, then it stands as only a monument of our own pride. May it be a useful tool as we seek to worship God and serve His people."

Reverend John Bartko came to Ecorse Presbyterian Church in 1972 and served faithfully until he died suddenly in 1993. During his pastorate, Ecorse experienced steady unemployment, "urban flight," declining property values and erosion of the public school system and youth recreational opportunities. Ecorse went into receivership from 1986 to 1990, and church membership fell to about 200 people as compared to 280 in 1979.

The Serbian Orthodox Church, with members shown here, has been located in Ecorse since the 1960s.

After the death of Reverend Bartko, temporary supply pastors served the church until 2002, when Reverend E. Dickson Forsyth was called out of retirement to serve the Ecorse Presbyterian Church. Over the last twenty years, the Ecorse Presbyterian Church has focused on being a "family church" with little emphasis on active outreach. As the community changed and members of the church family moved on or died, the congregation steadily declined to about seventy-one members. Sunday school enrollment suffered similar losses, and pledges and contributions also declined, eventually forcing the church to tap into its endowment and investment reserves. The energy and guidance of Reverend Forsyth revived a hopeful spirit in the hearts and minds of the remaining Ecorse Presbyterian Church members.

Then, in the winter of 2006, the remaining church members voted to merge with the Lincoln Park Presbyterian Church. A one-hundred-year-old Ecorse tradition ended on December 31, 2006, but the legacy of the Ecorse Presbyterian Church lives on in the hearts and minds of the thousands of individuals and families who grew physically, mentally and spiritually under its sheltering walls.

The Ecorse Baptist Temple sponsored a school, which operated in Ecorse for many years, as well as a church.

The Salvation Army, the Gospel Tabernacle, the Church of God, Mount Zion Baptist, First Baptist, the Episcopal and the Spiritualist Church joined the Presbyterians and the original St. Francis to create a network of churches in Ecorse.

CHAPTER 6

ECORSE GROWS AND CHANGES

At the turn of the twentieth century, Ecorse remained primarily a resort area and one of the early commuter suburbs for people working in Detroit. In 1903, the unincorporated village of Grandport became the largest village in the United States, and A.M. Salliotte was elected its first president.

The *Detroit Free Press* of July 2, 1905, described Ecorse:

> *All along the river shores from Fort Wayne to the Village of Ecorse, some hardier folks of Detroit who like to keep cool cheaply have boat houses in which they lived during the summer. "The Little Venice of the West End," they call it, and it is truly a colony of resorters distinct in itself. The rich may go to Grosse Point, to the mountains or to the sea shore; those of limited means, such as skilled mechanics, clerks and other small salaried men with families may easily afford to rent a cottage built out upon the piers of Ecorse's "Little Venice." There they may have the air and the cool of the river, in fact, all the real luxuries of a more exclusive colony and at much less cost. Every day the resorters of Ecorse who have business in the city travel back and forth on the trolley. And every evening they fish, boat and bathe with the women and children before the very doors of their summer homes.*

Although it was a rural and resort area, Ecorse attracted industrial barons like George Fink because of its river geography, natural resources and growing labor force. Ecorse had begun to build an industrial base. The Great Lakes Engineering Works Shipyard, located on the former Campau family farm and among the filled-in Detroit River marshes, gave Ecorse a swift industrial shove into the twentieth-century world of industry. In

Some Ecorse citizens of the 1920s and 1930s.

November 1904, the Pittsburgh Steamship Company, the lake fleet division of the United States Steel Corporation, was considering selling a number of small boats from its fleet. Several of them could be transferred to the coast before the present navigational season, and the deal was expected to be closed before Thanksgiving. The fleet managers were anxious to dispose of all of the whalebacks in the fleet because of the small profit margin in operating medium-sized carriers in the lake trade.

Harry Coulby, the president and general manager of the Pittsburgh Steamship Company, placed an order with the American Shipbuilding Company for four freighters with dimensions exceeding anything on the Great Lakes. The existing Pittsburgh Steamship Company fleet consisted of 112 vessels, and their carrying capacity in months of good dispatch was 1,500,000 tons, with a general average of 12,000,000 tons, allowing for fluctuation in seasons and other variables like weather.

United States Steel was motivated to modernize its Great Lakes fleet so it could make the optimum profit from the transportation end of the business, and according to a *Detroit Free Press* story, "It must be admitted that in the work of modernizing its fleet it occupies a most unique position because it is naturally unaffected by the price of steel. It will doubtless see that its own plate is supplied for its own ships."

Just over a year later, on the afternoon of December 3, 1905, despite the cold temperature, a large crowd watched the *B.F. Jones* leave the ways of the Ecorse yard of the Great Lakes Engineering Works. Miss Adelaide Dalzell Jones, daughter of B.F. Jones Jr. of Pittsburgh, sponsored the ship.

Mr. and Mrs. B.F. Jones, Miss Adelaide Dalzell Jones, Master B.F. Jones III, Mr. and Mrs. Willis L. King Jr. and Master Gordon King all attended from Pittsburgh. C.D. Wetherbee, general superintendent from Bath Ironworks

In the fifty-nine years between 1902 and 1961, the Great Lakes Engineering Works Ecorse shipyard built most of the large freighters in the Great Lakes fleet.

The Great Lakes Engineering Works Ecorse shipyard built over three hundred ships and employed as many as two thousand local workers when multimillion-dollar vessels needed to be built.

in Bath, Maine, attended, as did F.A. Goodrich from St. Louis, Missouri, and Arthur Cowlen Olahan from Philadelphia. Mr. Dunbar from Durango, Colorado, sat on the platform to watch the launching, as did Detroiters Mr. and Mrs. F.H. Holt, Mrs. Antonio C. Pessano, Miss Elizabeth Pessano, Miss Abbie Russel, Mrs. W.P. Hamilton, R.E. Plumb, W.S. Kinnear, W.S. Kinnear, Walter Russel, Antonio C. Pessano and John R. Russel. Congressman Edwin Denby was also part of the group of dignitaries watching the launchings.

The *B.F. Jones* was of the ten-thousand-ton class of ore boat, 550 feet long overall and 530 feet on the keel, 56 feet beam and 31 feet deep. Its equipment consisted of two Scotch boilers and triple expansion engines capable of developing two thousand horsepower. It was patterned after the other vessels on the drawing board of the Great Lakes Engineering Company scheduled for delivery the next year and was the first vessel of the fleet that the Jones

& Laughlin Steel Company placed on the lakes to match the fleet of the United States Steel Company and the Pittsburgh Steamship Company. The Jones & Laughlin Company now had five-year contracts under which its ore was transported down the lakes, and its purpose was to bring out vessels at a rate rapid enough to care for this tonnage in its own bottoms when the present contract was fulfilled.

As Great Lakes Engineering Works continued to turn out ships, Ecorse officials and ordinary citizens continued to struggle with the transition from rural village to industrial city. In her memoir about visiting Ecorse in the 1920s and 1930s, Dorothy Cummins Dunlop, a descendant of the Salliotte family that was one of the founding families of Ecorse, wrote that she and her family would travel to Ecorse from their attractive Detroit neighborhood in their old Hupmobile and that the "air was heavily polluted and retained a distressing odor."

Her grandfather, Joseph Salliotte, lived in a house on Jefferson Avenue in Ecorse with a view of the river from the porch. She wrote that the porch also included a "rather ugly commercial looking dock, bordered on each side by two dubious looking structures, one a saloon named the Polar Bear Café and on the south side of the dock was a fish market with large glass tanks. The existence of these two edifices made me question the acceptability of Ecorse as my ancestral home."

In 1923, the Michigan Steelworks plant was built on Mill Street, just inside the Ecorse-Wyandotte city limits off West Jefferson, and in 1930, Great Lakes Steel (now National Steel) established its Ecorse plant near the Great Lakes Engineering Works on the Detroit River. Michigan Steel was built at the dawning of the era when the American steel industry had begun to expand to meet increasing consumer demands.

George E. Fink, a former salesman for the West Penn Steel Company, Tarenton, Pennsylvania, and several other friends formed the Michigan Steel Corporation, and it was granted a charter in 1922. The original plant consisted of eight single stand mills, with six to be supplemented with soft mills. A machine shop, electric shop, carpenter shop, grease house and general labor building completed the complex. Production began on July 5, 1923, and the mill showed a profit from the beginning because a constant demand for quality steel kept the plant in full operation. Its success led to the idea and implementation of Great Lakes Steel Corporation in 1929 and the 1931 acquisition of Hanna Furnace blast furnace operations at Zug Island in 1931.

By the 1920s, Ecorse factories included Great Lakes Steel Corporation, Nicholson Terminal Dock Company, Great Lakes Engineering, Murray

These 1920s-era Ecorse hunters had to travel away from Ecorse to find beer and deer, but there were still plenty of muskrat in Ecorse Creek and the Detroit River.

Body Corporation, Grassnell Chemical Company, DT&I Roundhouse, National Smelting Company, Schwayder Brothers Manufacturing Company, Wolverine Varnish Company, Michigan Steel Corporation, Ryan Foundry and Modern Collett & Machine Company.

George Fink, who founded the Michigan Steel Company as well as the Great Lakes Steel Corporation, was a true son of the steel industry. As a salesman for the Western Pennsylvania Steel Company, he recognized the tremendous potential of the Ecorse location—raw materials, fuel, accessibility, markets and manpower were all there. He believed that coal could be shipped in by boat from the southeast and iron ore from the north and that the growing automobile industry would provide a ready market. The Depression (the founding year of Great Lakes Steel was 1929) would provide the workers from the many area unemployed. To finance his Michigan Steel Company and later Great Lakes Steel, George Fink raised $1 million and began Michigan Steel in 1922. He developed an unusual policy so he could raise funds without subscription or recourse to municipal bonds. The company paid no percentage, no fees and no stock bonuses; stock was sold at fifty dollars per share to everyone; and all monies were applied to the business. Using the same methods, George Fink launched Great Lakes Steel in March 1929 with $20 million in funding.

By the summer of 1929, the skeletons of three huge steel barns, 1,550 feet long, stood over the swamp; then something happened to ensure the company's future. Ernest T. Weir of West Virginia's Weirton Steel Company came forward with an idea for a merger. Fink accepted the idea, and the joining of Weirton, a small but very profitable company, with Great Lakes laid the foundation for National Steel. Then George Humphrey, director of Cleveland's M.A. Hanna Company, arrived on the scene. Hanna Company owned more than 150 million tons of high-grade iron ore reserves in Minnesota's Mesabi Range and was willing to sell the raw material to independent steel manufacturers. National needed a sure supply of ore, and Humphrey and Hanna, the last major independent suppliers, were eager to fill the void. Besides the ore, National acquired the company's blast furnaces on Zug Island and the ownership of some of Hanna's Michigan mines.

The new Great Lakes Steel buildings were constructed on reclaimed swampland with 3.5 million cubic feet of sand from Lake St. Clair distributed over the marshlands. A total of seventy-two thousand piles were driven down more than seventy feet to bedrock, and the first mill was built on that foundation. The plants of the Great Lakes Steel Corporation began operations in August 1930 and have continued ever since. National Steel invested another $16 million in the plant during the first year to make sure that it got off to a good start, and during that first year, Great Lakes rolled out 500,000 tons of sheet steel and paid $13 million to Ecorse and River Rouge in municipal and school taxes.

During World War II, Great Lakes Steel became one of the nation's largest producers of armor plate, with the Michigan Steel Plant playing a major role in the final processing of the plates prior to shipment. Michigan Steel also produced other wartime matériel such as forty-foot naval Quonset huts, nose hangars, barracks, steel for powder magazines, camouflage frames for gun mounts and arch ribs for naval warehouse buildings.

Ecorse industry and shipbuilding helped America win World War II. Great Lakes Steel manufactured steel and steel products; Great Lakes Engineering ships and Modern Collett and other industries contributed much to war production. Immigration from outside and migration from within the United States swelled the population of Ecorse. Hungarian, Greek, Polish and Italian people settled in and around Ecorse during World War II. Thousands of white and black people from the South came north to work in the automobile and other industries and built lives in Ecorse and the Down River area. In these years, people found Ecorse a good place to raise a family, and the population swelled to a peak of about nineteen thousand people. Ecorse became a city in 1942, and although it was plagued by turbulent politics, cronyism and fiscal problems, business and civic affairs flourished.

Sandy Blakeman was one of the premier Ecorse photographers and businessmen. He and his wife, Mary, were lifelong Ecorse boosters.

In the mid-1950s, a well-known Ecorse photographer and businessman, M. Sandy Blakeman, interviewed several Ecorse civic and business leaders and wrote their stories for the *Mellus Newspapers*. In 1955, Blakeman interviewed Paul Carnahan, the president of Great Lakes Steel Corporation. Blakeman wrote:

> *The dynamic personality of Paul Carnahan is expressed, not pretentiously, but in a conservative soft-spoken manner. One immediately senses the strength of purpose of a man who is pleasant yet forthright in expressing his opinion. When asked how he feels about industry and its position as a leading force in Ecorse, he commented, "Industry can be a good citizen, just as you and I."*
>
> *His interest in community matters on a smaller scale is shown by the company's active support in a project for youth-junior achievement. With Great Lakes as one of the "spark plugs," several industries and businesses are providing funds and personnel to sponsor a center for Downriver boys and girls where they can operate their own companies and thus gain experience in all phases of business of their own choosing.*
>
> *Most associates refer to him as a "Downriver-minded" man. He first became affiliated with the Great Lakes Steel Corporation in 1934. He began as an hourly wage employee in the blooming mill in the slab transfer operation. He rose through the ranks and was promoted to director in charge of production in 1953. His next promotion was to vice-president in charge of sales and in April he was elected senior vice-president of the company. When George R. Fink retired from the company's presidency on May 25, 1954, Carnahan was elected to succeed him. Few men are more familiar with the problems of downriver communities than Paul Carnahan and it is plain that he sincerely believes that industry can—and should—be a good citizen.*

Ecorse Grows and Changes

In the 1960s, under its parent company, National Steel Company, Great Lakes Steel manufactured 31 percent of the company's total production. The company produced steel for traditional uses, and steel remains its focal point, but it expanded into new areas of production, as well, including home furnishings, appliances and steel frames for home construction. Great Lakes also produced crushed slag for use in road construction. At its peak, the company employed nearly twelve thousand men and shipped 4.5 million tons of steel annually.

By the 1970s, production at Michigan Steel had been limited to heat treatment processing of steel plates, although there were several other vital and ultramodern company departments located within the plant boundaries. A small staff of security and general labor employees, the hourly and salaried payroll departments, management services and primary accounting and computer operations departments also occupied the buildings. By turn of the twenty-first century, Michigan Steel had ceased its operations, and the buildings were being demolished so that a condominium complex could be built where workers once labored to produce steel that helped win World War II.

Downsizing and reduced production marked the last decades of the twentieth century at Great Lakes Steel, but in the early twenty-first century, the Ecorse and River Rouge plants were still productive and vigorous and still a major employer in the Down River area.

Ellis Duke Underill operated the Underill Insurance agency in Ecorse, belonged to the Ecorse Businessman's Association and contributed heavily to the health and wealth of the community. He loved Ecorse so much that he requested before his death that he be buried in tiny Ecorse Cemetery, owned by St. Francis Xavier Church. Born in Syracuse, New York, on July 10, 1892, Duke came to live in Ecorse as a boy. After serving with the Marine Corps in the First World War, he returned to Ecorse and entered the real estate and insurance fields. He founded Underill Insurance Agency about 1921, and from that office through the years he and his coworkers handled the insurance needs of banks, corporations, municipalities and school districts. He operated his agency until 1968, when he retired and sold the business to his brother-in-law and longtime business associate Frank Butler. Even though he retired, he continued to visit the office and offer advice. During the 1920s, when Ecorse began to grow into a thriving city, Duke worked with other real estate developers in plotting streets and subdivisions throughout the community. He was such an Ecorse booster that Mayor William W. Voisine gave him the title of "Goodwill Ambassador" for the city, a title that he held until his death. He bragged about Ecorse, calling it "the greatest little city in the world."

Duke Underrill, left, was an Ecorse businessman and booster, though not necessarily in that order. He was also famous for his hat wardrobe.

Born in Ecorse in 1897, Ormal Goodell was the great-grandson of Civil War veteran Elijah Goodell. Ormal established Goodell Hardware Company and became a respected community leader.

Ecorse Grows and Changes

When he wasn't working, he loved to hunt and fish, especially along the Detroit River. When he died in 1973, the old St. Francis Cemetery, which didn't see burials often, was crowded with people who came to say goodbye to Duke as he was granted his last wish. Ecorse citizens like Duke Ellis and Sandy Blakeman thought of Ecorse in a fond, positive way, and in so thinking they influenced the personality of Ecorse.

Ecorse, John Duguay and the *Edmund Fitzgerald*

Along with Sandy Blakeman, John Duguay was one of the premier photographers recording Ecorse history in the 1950s. John had a special interest in the Great Lakes Engineering Works Shipyard in Ecorse. Great Lakes Engineering had built its Hull 1, the *Fontana*, in 1905, and it was still in service on the Great Lakes. Workers in the shipyards built vessels for the Great Lakes and repaired and converted existing vessels for ocean service in both world wars. They built ore carriers and other famous ships, such as the state ferry *Vacationland*, right up until 1969. John followed the building history of the Great Lakes Engineering Works, and he especially enjoyed photographing the *Edmund Fitzgerald*.

Alex Petrie, left, served on the Ecorse City Council; close friend John Duguay's photography of Ecorse provides an important historical record for the city.

On February 1, 1957, the Northwestern Mutual Insurance Company of Milwaukee signed a contract with the Great Lakes Engineering Works of Ecorse to build the first super freighter on the Great Lakes. By August 7, 1957, workers at the shipyard at the Great Lakes Engineering Works laid the keel of the 729-foot ore carrier. Initially known as *Hull 301*, it would be the largest ore carrier on the Great Lakes. Besides *Hull 301*, the Great Lakes Shipyard workers also labored on another 729-foot ore carrier for the Bethlehem Steel Corporation and a 696-foot freighter for the Interlake Steamship Company.

According to Hugh McElroy, general superintendent of the Great Lakes Engineering Works, building the three vessels would provide employment for approximately 1,300 workers for the next three years and triple the company's workforce. He said that work would begin on the other two ships before *Hull 301* was finished. Hugh McElroy and other officials of Great Lakes Engineering and the Columbia Transportation Company, which was slated to operate the $7 million vessel for twenty-seven years, watched a giant crane swing the keel plate into place. Charles Haskill, president of the Great Lakes Engineering Works, and Fred R. White Jr. of Cleveland, executive vice-president of the Columbia Transportation Company division of the Oglebay Norton Company, officiated at the brief ceremony that preceded the laying of the first portion of the keel. The ship was commissioned by the Northwestern Mutual Life Insurance Company of Milwaukee.

The giant ship, designed for Great Lakes and Seaway shipping, was slated to be launched early in the spring of 1958. It was to be constructed of prefabricated steel subassemblies, the first prefabrication ever done on a large lake vessel. This was a radical departure from past shipbuilding procedures in which the keel was laid first, then other bottom plates and then the sides and interior were built up piece by piece. *Hull 301* would have a seventy-five-foot molded depth and have the carrying capacity of approximately 26,800 long tons of iron ore. It would be thirteen feet longer than any vessel currently afloat on the Great Lakes.

Over the next nine months, John Duguay monitored the progress of the giant ship as it took shape on the ways. By Thursday, June 12, 1958, the *Ecorse Advertiser* reported the story of the launching of the *Edmund Fitzgerald*, which had taken place on Saturday, June 7, 1958, and John was one of the crowd of over fifteen thousand people who flocked to the launching at Great Lakes Engineering Works. (There is an ongoing discussion about whether the *Edmund Fitzgerald* was launched in River Rouge or in Ecorse because part of Great Lake's Engineering Shipyards were located within River Rouge boundaries. No matter where the launch took place, it was constructed in Ecorse.)

Ecorse Grows and Changes

Spectators overflowed the reviewing stands erected for the launching ceremonies, and as the gigantic ship dropped sideways into the Detroit River, Mrs. Edmund Fitzgerald—wife of the chairman of the Northwestern Mutual Life Insurance Company—smashed a bottle of champagne on its bow. People cheered as the 729-foot ship slid gently down greased ways into a 150-foot-wide slip at 12:00 p.m., creating a huge wave against the opposite shore.

The blasts of tugs, seven freighters, whistles from small craft and industries along the riverfront and the cheers of about 250 pleasure boaters mingled with the cheers of the spectators as the *Edmund Fitzgerald* rocked in the water. Airliners, military craft and two helicopters circled overhead. Shipyard veterans remembered it as the loudest and longest salute to a launching that they had ever experienced. According to the *Ecorse Advertiser*, it was "the biggest side launching ever held in the world."

John took several photographs of the *Edmund Fitzgerald* during its launching, and he and countless other Down River citizens watched its graceful progress up and down the Detroit River over the years.

The *Edmund Fitzgerald's* beauty, length, cargo carrying capacity and human fan club combined to make it "the pride of the American side." During the 1960s, its longtime master, Captain Peter Pulcer, helped make it

John Duguay took several pictures of the *Edmund Fitzgerald* from the Great Lakes Engineering Works shipyard in Ecorse.

more popular by performing various antics to entertain people as the "big *Fitz*" glided down the rivers and lakes. He would salute people who might be watching his ship with whistle blasts, and he would play music on the PA system so that everyone on shore could hear it. While passing through the Soo locks and narrow rivers like the Detroit and St. Clair, he would broadcast facts about the *Fitzgerald* with a bullhorn. The *Fitz* set a number of cargo records over the years and proved to be extremely seaworthy. Besides the stiffening of hull members, installing a bow thruster in 1969, converting to oil fuel and fitting automated boiler controls over the winter of 1971–72 were the only major work that the *Edmund Fitzgerald* ever needed.

"She was a beautiful ship and she was strong," John remembers, with the look of Great Lakes horizons in his eye.

For seventeen years, the *Fitz* steamed stalwartly through the Great Lakes, taking storms and taconite pellets in its stride. Then, as dawn broke on November 10, 1975, a massive low-pressure system moved northwest from Escanaba, Michigan. As it moved across Lake Superior, it whipped the waters into monstrous waves with foaming crests. Captain Ernst McSorley, now master of the *Edmund Fitzgerald*, had accumulated over forty years of experience on the Great Lakes, but this storm made him wary. He left Superior, Wisconsin, with a load of 26,116 tons of taconite pellets to be delivered to Zug Island near Ecorse, charting his course within ten miles of the *Arthur M. Anderson* of the United States Steel Corporation's Great Lakes Fleet so that they could navigate seething Lake Superior together.

As the storm increased in intensity that afternoon, Captain McSorley called Captain Cooper of the *Arthur M. Anderson* and reported that the *Fitz* had lost two vent covers and some railing and was taking on water and listing. He asked Captain Cooper for a radar fix because his radar had failed. Darkness set in and snow squalls made the *Fitz* nearly invisible. At 7:10 p.m. Captain Cooper called Captain McSorley to check on the condition of the *Fitz*. Captain McSorley replied, "We are holding our own."

Fifteen minutes later, as the *Anderson* emerged from a snow squall, Cooper couldn't believe what he *wasn't* seeing. The *Edmund Fitzgerald* had disappeared from sight and sound. Captain Cooper couldn't see it visually or on radar and couldn't contact it by radio. Captain Cooper called the Coast Guard to report that "the *Fitz* is gone."

Three days later, a navy helicopter and the Coast Guard found the wreckage of the *Edmund Fitzgerald* approximately seventeen miles from the entrance to Whitefish Bay in 535 feet of water. A 276-foot section of the bow sat upright, and a 253 foot section of the stern lay inverted about 170 feet away—in between lay piles of taconite pellets.

Ecorse Grows and Changes

The mystery of what sank the *Edmund Fitzgerald* seems to lie as deep as the *Fitzgerald* itself. What forces of nature could sink a ship its size so quickly? None of the men aboard it sent flares or an SOS. The ship just disappeared. If Captain McSorley had managed to bring it over those last few miles, it would have been safe in calmer water, but all twenty-nine of its crew members, including Captain McSorley, who had commanded it since 1972, were lost. None of their bodies ever washed ashore from the wreck.

On August 2, 1977, the Coast Guard released a report saying that the *Fitzgerald* sank because of faulty hatch covers. Many people were not satisfied with this report, and over the years many controversial theories about the sinking of the *Edmund Fitzgerald* have been put forth. Some people say that the *Fitz* could have bottomed out or grounded near Six Fathom Shoal, which supposedly was not mapped correctly. Others contend that the crew may not have securely fastened the clamps that held down the hatches, allowing water to seep in. Others contend that the hatches themselves were faulty. According to some, the *Fitz* had previous structural damage that had not been properly repaired, and the adverse conditions of the storm made the damage worse and caused it to sink. Some people say that enormous waves, called the "Three Sisters," swamped and sank the *Fitz*. Many others think that a monstrous wave could have buried the *Fitz* and pushed its front under water, causing it to hit ground and break in two. Others say that the waves lifted the bow and stern of the *Fitz* but could not hold the center of the ship that contained the cargo. The overload pushed the center down, sinking the *Fitz* and breaking it in two.

The crew and the *Edmund Fitzgerald* itself are remembered in the minds and hearts of people who loved them both. On July 4, 1995, the ship's bell was recovered from the wreck and now reposes in the Great Lakes Shipwreck Museum in Whitefish Point. An anchor that the *Fitz* lost on an earlier trip was recovered from the Detroit River and is displayed at the Dossin Great Lakes Museum in Detroit. The Museum Ship, *Steamship Valley Camp*, in Sault Ste. Marie holds some *Fitzgerald* artifacts, including Lifeboat 2, which is shredded like paper, some photos and commemorative models and paintings.

One of the Ecorse shipyard workers who helped build the *Fitz* doesn't remember it as being quite as strong as John Duguay remembered. Requesting to remain anonymous, he remarked that he and several of the other men who worked on it felt that it was not seaworthy because of inferior riveting and incorrect placement of some of the prefabricated parts. In fact, he thinks that the way the *Fitzgerald* was built made it ultimately unseaworthy.

John Duguay gravely considered the mystery and speculation surrounding the *Edmund Fitzgerald*. Then he smiled. "I took pictures of her," he said. "That is a good way to honor her."

Renaissance on the Rivers

In July 1958, seventy-year-old Eli "Peck" LeBlanc officially retired from a fifteen-year stint as Ecorse dog warden. A descendant of one of the Down River area's oldest families, he still lived at 4560 West Jefferson in a home built on the site of the original farm that the Pottawatomie Indians had deeded to his great-grandfather Pierre in 1790 when he came to Ecorse from France.

LeBlanc was born on August 10, 1888, in a house on West Jefferson that was razed in 1957. The LeBlanc homestead, which was located on the site of his present home, is 105 years old and was moved to Webster Street. Abraham LeBlanc, Peck's grandfather, owned four farms, covering acres of land in Ecorse and Lincoln Park. The original farm extended from LeBlanc to White and from the Detroit River back to Ecorse Creek, now River Drive. His other farms were located on land that today comprises most of the south end of Lincoln Park.

In 1904, when he was sixteen, LeBlanc worked in an icehouse on the Detroit River, cutting huge blocks of ice that were then stored in sawdust to use during the summer months. At this time, he was attending the old school, which was razed in 1910 to make way for the "new" school, which is now Ecorse School Two. When he was a young blade of seventeen, Peck decided that it was time he had a "regular" suit. He got a job at the Great

The Detroit River is one of the busiest waterways and anchorages on the Great Lakes.

Ecorse Grows and Changes

Lakes Engineering Works in Ecorse as a fitter's helper and worked for five months until he had enough money to buy his new suit. "I remember I paid $15 for a blue serge suit, and then shopped around a bit before buying my first watch. It was a $25 gem," he recalled.

Trained as a railroad telegraph operator in 1906, LeBlanc spent most of his adult working life following the trade. Lured by the call of the clicking key, he traveled most of Michigan finding jobs as telegrapher at stations in Vanderbilt, Mackinaw, Roscommon, Indian River and many other places before settling down at the Michigan Central' s Wyandotte station.

In 1908, he transferred to the Ecorse station on Southfield and remained there until 1915, shortly before the station was closed to make way for the Southfield viaduct. After a short stay at the Rockwood station, he changed careers for a time and served as a timekeeper in the old Ecorse Foundry and the Detroit Brass and Malleable in Wyandotte. During World War I, he worked as a timekeeper at the Wyandotte shipyards.

The last ship launched at Great Lakes Engineering Works, the *Arthur Homer*, slid down the ways of the works in Ecorse on November 7, 1959. At the time of its launching, the carrier was the biggest ship on the Great Lakes, and its launching was the largest side launching in maritime history. The *Homer* out measured the *Edmund Fitzgerald*, then the "Queen of the Lakes," by one foot.

During the 1920s, William LaJoie operated the Riverview Hotel, which was located on the Detroit River.

Turning his attention to politics, LeBlanc served as assistant town marshal in Ecorse from 1916 to 1917 under George Moore. He recalled that he provided his own motorcycle, riding along West Jefferson as he chased speeding motorists. He also paid for gasoline, oil and bike repairs. His only pay during that time was the $3.75 that he collected for each ticket that he issued. Speeders were usually fined $10.00, with the judge receiving $4.75, the arresting officer getting his share and the remainder going into the village coffers. To earn extra money, Peck chased speeders in Ford City, which later merged with Wyandotte. He still enjoyed riding his motorcycle through city traffic.

In 1929, he continued his telegraphy career at the Wyandotte station of the Detroit, Toledo and Ironton Railroad, working there for ten years until he assumed the position of chief clerk in the traffic department. He left in 1943 to become dog warden in Ecorse.

LeBlanc and his wife, Ruth, celebrated their thirty-fifth wedding anniversary in June 1958. They had five sons: Reggie, Herby, Jim, Jack and Larry, and a daughter, Margaret. LeBlanc and his first wife, Leona Yops, who died in 1921, were parents of a son, Donald, and a daughter, Fern.

For years, Peck spent most of his free time sitting on the front porch of his home on Jefferson Avenue and gazing through his binoculars at the mighty

Ecorse Grows and Changes

President Lyndon Baines Johnson was one of the many public figures who visited Ecorse. Others included Eleanor Roosevelt and Dr. Martin Luther King Jr.

ships that passed back and forth on the Detroit River. All of the freighter captains knew him, and he kept track of them by subscribing to various marine magazines.

Fourteen years later, even though he was retired, Peck had not retired his binocular surveillance of his beloved river. In May 1972, the *Stewart Cort*, at the time the largest ship ever to sail the Great Lakes or on the Detroit River, made a pass up the Detroit River right by Peck's house. He had been anxiously waiting for the *Cort* for several months. When Peck discovered that the Bethlehem Steel Corporation had built the *Cort*, which measured one thousand feet, and that it would pass his house, he planned to sit on the front porch and get a good look at it. It was upbound on the river on its maiden voyage from Erie, Pennsylvania, where it was built, heading to Lake Superior to take on nearly fifty-two thousand tons of iron ore. Its regular route was scheduled to run between Taconite Harbor, Minnesota, north of Duluth, and Bethlehem's mill at Burns Harbor, east of Gary, Indiana. It was unlikely that it would ever again pass through the Detroit River.

Above: Ann Coman, the wife of former mayor George Coman.

Left: Peter Johnson was one of two black veterans elected to the Ecorse City Council in the late 1950s.

Ecorse Grows and Changes

To make the occasion more special for Peck, the *Cort* blinked a special "Hi Peck" as the ship passed his house. When the public relations people at Bethlehem Steel heard that Peck would be watching for the ship, they said yes to the request. With his telegraphy training, Peck had no trouble understanding the greeting.

The *Cort* had been expected to pass the Down River area the week before but had been delayed from leaving Erie, Pennsylvania, because of icy conditions in Lakes Huron and Superior. When the *Cort* reached Sault Ste. Marie, it passed through the lock under its own power with only two and a half feet to spare on each side. It spent most of its days above Lake Ontario because it was too big for Canada's Welland Canal, between Lakes Erie and Ontario, or for any of the St. Lawrence Seaway locks.

Peck's life parallels the life of Ecorse after World War II. For decades after World War II, Ecorse grew and prospered along with the rest of the United States. After World War II, a housing shortage sparked a largely middle-class mushrooming of the American suburbs. With their GI Bill loans for

Ecorse mayor Dick Manning greets Detroit mayor Jerome Cavanaugh.

Another political gathering in Ecorse.

housing, farms and businesses in hand, American GIs married and began to raise families, and several developers seized the opportunity and applied the principles of mass production to build identical houses on modest lots. They sold some of these homes to professionals in middle management, some to the lower middle class and some to working-class people. Wages from the automobile companies in Detroit and United States Steel in Ecorse helped workers finance homes in Ecorse and the rest of the Down River suburbs.

Ecorse Grows and Changes

Ecorse officials at a 1970s waterfront celebration.

During the 1960s, 1970s and 1980s, the negative underside of Ecorse life began to change its physical and demographic nature. As the riots and social unrest of the 1960s affected the Detroit metropolitan area, people began to leave Ecorse for the outer ring of suburbs in Ecorse Township and Oakland County. Ecorse suffered the same urban problems that most of America has suffered in the past decades. The "white flight" to the suburbs, urban decline and political and social unrest of the 1970s, 1980s and 1990s drastically affected Ecorse, and because of its geographic limitations and declining population, the city had a difficult time surviving. Although it has had many capable politicians who have served the community loyally and well, Ecorse also has endured corrupt politicians and wasteful spending that adversely affected its municipal government.

In December 1986, Ecorse became the first city in Michigan to declare bankruptcy, with a $6 million deficit. The Wayne County Circuit Court issued a court order that appointed Louis Schimmel receiver for the bankrupt city, now with a population of just twelve thousand. The court gave him authority to replace the elected mayor and city council members and set the city finances back on course.

Two mayors: Eli Cuingun (right) and William Voisine.

Mayor Richard Manning of Ecorse meeting Michigan governor George Romney in the late 1970s.

Over the four years that Schimmel acted as receiver, he privatized nearly all of the city's services. He negotiated contacts with the police and firefighter's unions that saved money and made the departments more efficient. He privatized the Department of Public Works, saving Ecorse over $1 million per year. His mandatory, stringent financial policies and management practices got Ecorse back on its financial feet and earned him national recognition as a man of action who was unafraid to implement the tough measures

Ecorse Grows and Changes

Political campaigns in Ecorse were not just campaigns; they were gala events and opportunities to socialize.

Sometimes politicians in Ecorse have been corrupt, but there have also been many dedicated and loyal public servants.

necessary to save a city. Schimmel's four-year receiver term ended in 1990, but he remained as official watchdog of Ecorse until August 1, 1999. That year, the Wayne County Circuit Court's management supervision of the City of Ecorse formally came to an end.

In later years, Schimmel said that for the most part Ecorse has followed the financial practices that he implemented. He said that if Ecorse keeps its financial house in order and doesn't backslide into mismanagement, it has a bright future.

Ann Coman (wife of former mayor George Coman), her daughter, JoAnn, and her grandchildren.

Meetings were inescapable events in the civic and church life of Ecorse.

Ecorse Grows and Changes

Celebrations, both political and otherwise, are at the forefront of Ecorse life.

A reelection campaign event for James Tassis (right), who was mayor of Ecorse from 1989 to 2001.

In the conclusion of her memoir, Dorothy Cummins Dunlop cited articles about development plans for Ecorse and the Down River area, plans that she and her family supported. She said that she was especially pleased that the development agency targeted 120 acres of land at the foot of Southfield Road in Ecorse, the former site of her grandfather's old wood house and the former site of the Polar Bear Café, the dock and the fish market. She concluded that "perhaps the second millennium will fulfill the dream that the first settlers of Ecorse and all of those who have lived there since that living so intimately with such a great river could only bring success and happiness."

CHAPTER 7

FOUR FRENCHMEN FROM ECORSE FORGE THE ECORSE ROWING CLUB'S FUTURE

E ver since Indians and French voyagers paddled canoes down the green waters of the Detroit River to the Ecorse Creek centuries ago, Ecorse has been a maritime community. This maritime heritage has forged the social, economic and political destinies of Ecorse and other Down River communities and shaped the personalities of both native and immigrant citizens. Rowing and regattas were and still are an important part of the maritime history of Ecorse and the other Down River communities that maritime historians often overlook. The history of rowing is woven into the history of Ecorse and the Ecorse Boat Club.

In the early 1870s, Four Frenchmen wearing red plaid checkered shirts and blue overall jeans rowed in a ten-oared barge down Ecorse Creek to its mouth at the Detroit River. The Montie brothers were on the way to transforming Ecorse from a rural French hamlet into a town of international renown and respect. Ecorse in the 1870s was a tiny hamlet perched along a two-mile stretch of the Detroit River. The 1873 business directory included a salon, grocery stores, a hotel, a brickyard, a feed store, J.B. Montie, blacksmith, a shoemaker, a butcher and John Copeland's sawmill.

The names of some of the first rowers and generations of championship rowers also appear on the 1876 map as owners of farms and land near Ecorse Creek. They include Beaubien, LeBlanc, Champagne and Montie. Richard LeBlanc was one of the first to visualize the possibilities of a rowing club in Ecorse. He promoted the idea among his friends, and in 1873 they organized a rowing club of fewer than twenty members. They called their organization the Wah-Wah-Tah-See Club because Indian names were the general custom in those days.

Richard Montie, a member of the old ten-oared barge crew that his brothers sponsored in the 1870s, helped Richard LeBlanc organize the first club. Richard was the fifth of the ten children of John Baptiste Montie and Amelia Goodell Montie. His father John settled in Ecorse after leaving Quebec and married Amelia Goodell of Grosse Isle.

Gustave Raupp was another ethnic name that would play an important part in Ecorse rowing history. Gustave came to Ecorse Township with his father Matthias Sr. and brothers Matthias and Herman, first settling in Delray and later in Ecorse Township. Matthias Sr. bought a farm near Pepper Road at what is now Outer Drive and Dix. When he came of age, Gustave moved to the village of Grandport, where he and Alexis M. Salliotte founded the Salliotte & Raupp Lumber Company.

In 1901, Gustave guided a raft containing 2.5 million feet of pine, hemlock, spruce and tamarack logs coming down the St. Clair River for use in his mill. One of G.A. Raupp's other endeavors, the Ecorse Rowing Club, proved to be even more lasting than his mill, which went out of business in mid-century. He was one of its founding fathers and helped organize its first crew in 1873.

In 1882, the Monties' Wah-Wah-Tah-See teammates Charles Tank, Frank Seavitt, Lou Champaign and Elmer Labadie organized a crew, and from 1882 until 1887 they rowed and won several races. Other Ecorse men who rowed during these years and established records for the Ecorse Club included Theodore Bondie, Alfred Beaubien, Charles Sesyer, Bill McGullen, Bill Clement, George Clark, Alex Beaubien, Henry Lange, Gus Gramer (at times keeper of the Mamajuda and Grassy Island lights) and Mark Bourassa. These men rowed in four barges and entered both Junior and Senior races. George Clark built the first boat for the Ecorse Club and the club used it in practically all of its races.

The next year, on July 29, 1885, the Monties pitted their rowing skills against the Hillsdales in the Belle Isle Regatta. The Hillsdales had just won the Canadian Henley Regatta held at St. Catharines, Ontario, and crowds cheered them all along the Detroit River. The Wah-Wah-Ta-Sees nominated the Montie brothers to row against the retuning champions. The three contenders lined up at the starting line—the Montie brothers, the Hillsdales and the Centennials. The starting gun reported, and the Monties shot their Alger shell ahead of the Hillsdales, leaving them trailing ten feet.

At the turn in the course, the Montie brothers were two lengths ahead and rowing at the unprecedented stroke of sixty to the minute. The endurance of the Frenchmen enabled them to hold that phenomenal stroke to the end of the race. They finished four lengths ahead of the Hillsdales and nearly a half-mile ahead of the Centennials. Lige Montie summarized the race in his own words when he exclaimed that he and his brothers had "beat de Hillsdales dat was just back from Hingland."

The Ecorse Rowing Club's Future

On the day after the race, the four Monties were back on the Rouge River, wearing their blue-jean overalls and attending to their logging. On Sundays they would sit around old Alec Cicotte's place near the Rouge River, wearing their Sunday clothes, their coats covered with medals. They won many other races, but they most enjoyed talking about the one where they beat the Henley champions who had just returned from "Hingland."

Charles Tank on the River

Charles Tank was born in Ecorse in 1870, and by 1886 he had entered the four-oared shell of the old Ecorse Boat Club into contention. By 1891, he was coaching the club and rowing at the same time, and in 1893 he won his first Northwestern Regatta in Detroit. He also won the hand of Genevive Montie, who was the sister of the famous Montie brothers who had established the rowing tradition in Ecorse. She and Charles were married in 1893. In the 1890s, twelve-hour workdays at the shipyards and foundries were the lot of the ordinary workingman. In the summertime, when the working day ended, men who wanted to relax and enjoy the cooling river breezes or hand their wives a string of fresh fish for supper would take to the river in rowboats or barges. Charles worked to support Genevive and their family of four boys—Louis, William, Vernon and Charles—and a daughter, Mary.

Charles loved rowing. For seven years he rowed with the prize-winning crews of the 1890s. In 1893, the Ecorse crew consisted of Frank Salliotte, Elmer Labadie, Charles Tank and Theodore Beaubien. This crew remained intact through the 1894 season, but in 1895 Charles was the only member of the crew left to welcome Bill Clement, George Clark and Alex Beaubien.

In 1896, another Ecorse crew composed of Alex and Alfred Beaubien, Charles Tank, Charles Sesyer and Louis Champagne set a world's record for the one-and-a-half-mile race around one buoy. In 1897, the crew was made up of Charles Tank, Louis Champaign, Alfred and Alex Beaubien, and in 1898 Bill McGullin and Henry Lange joined the crew, as well as Albert J. Salliotte.

Just before the turn of the century, rowing regattas were popular, and the Wah-Wah-Tah-See Club entered every race it could. During these years, the Ecorse men consistently won in the Northwester on the Detroit River, Bay City, Orchard Lake, Lake St. Clair and at Monroe. Alvia Grant was among the famous Ecorse oarsmen just before the turn of the century. In 1901, at Orchard Lake, the Wah-Wah-Tah-Sees won easily with an entirely new crew consisting of Fred Vellmure, Frank Grant and Ignatius Salliotte pulling oars. Fred Vellmure was also the sculler for the Ecorse Boat Club. During these years, Ecorse defeated the Detroit Boat Club, Excelsior, Zypher and Centennial, all from Detroit. In a wider circle of victory they conquered Bay City, Port Huron, Battle Creek, Monroe, Chicago, Wyandotte, Saginaw and Windsor, Ontario.

The Rowing Club Reincarnated

As the Wah-Wah-Tah-Sees rowed into the twentieth century, they rowed against the hometown backdrop of a resort area and one of Detroit's earlier commuter suburbs. Summer cottage people and yearlong residents of Ecorse would often stroll down to the river and watch the rowers practice their runs.

The Ecorse Boat Club disbanded in 1906, and oarsmen from Ecorse raced under the Wyandotte Boat Club Banner. But the colorful memories of the Montie brothers kept alive the Ecorse tradition, and inevitably the grandsons of William Montie, the Tank brothers, served as the backbone of the reorganized Ecorse Club. After rowing with the title crews in the 1890s, Charles Tank watched the Ecorse Rowing Club disband for lack of competition. For seven years he coached the boys in these clubs, including his own sons, to win competitions and helped make the Ecorse Club one of the best in the country.

After the Ecorse Boat Club disbanded, Tank continued rowing alone, and in the mid-1930s, his sons Louis and William (Red) began to row for the Wyandotte Boat Club, where their father had coached them. Louis and Red won sculling event after event, and Tank's other sons, Vernon and Pete, were also involved in the club, Vernon as president and Pete as a topflight boatman. In 1938, when he was just eighteen, Louis defeated Morris Morton of the Detroit Boat Club in the sculling event and competed in Buffalo later in the season, winning several national club contests. Red also won considerable recognition as a rower in an eight-man shell, and he and Louis won the doubles event at the Canadian Henley at St. Catharines, Ontario, and James Cameron and Herb Beaubien won the Junior Doubles Championship.

According to Larry LeBlanc, one of the vintage rowers with the club, "Louis's forte was grace and that seeming lack of effort; Red was the fire and courage of their duo." The Tanks stored a single and double just south of Hogan's Alley in Ecorse—the infamous Hogan's Alley where rumrunners had come and gone with expensive cargos and the ordinary citizens of Ecorse had wrested bootleggers from the clutches of federal customs agents.

Charles Tank would often row by Hogan's Alley, and for another five years he continued to dream of resurrecting the Ecorse Boat Club. Finally it happened. In late 1938, before the 1939 season began, a meeting was held in the office of Ecorse Village official J.P. Alger (Doc) Salliotte. A nucleus of rowing enthusiasts met to form an Ecorse Rowing Club. Those charter members attending that meeting were Nelson Bolthouse; Jack Sharon; Bernie Seneski; Art Sims; Bob Carley; Nick Pappas; Don LeBlanc; Red, Louis, Pete, Mike and Charles Tank; Newt Goodell; Lambert Pfeiffer; Bob Brown; and Larry Smith. The first president was Mike Tank, the vice-president William J. (Tip) Goodell, the secretary Arthur Sims and the treasurer Ormal Goodell. Charles Tank was appointed coach. The reorganized Ecorse Boat Club started out with a $350 deficit for a note to purchase a secondhand eight-oar shell from the Detroit Boat Club. Charles Tank started out with the vintage shell—built in 1910—and large amounts of faith and courage.

The newly organized club quickly purchased another shell and christened the two shells *Genevive Tank* and *George R. Fink*. The *Ecorse Tribune* said in 1938 that "it was largely through Mrs. Tank's efforts that the Ecorse Boat Club was revived last year." George R. Fink was the founder of the Michigan Steel Corporation and later Great Lakes (National Steel). However, a tornado whipped through the Down River area that spring, nearly destroying what the new club had begun to build.

The building first used as a club was the old brick building at the south end of Riverside Park that was formerly an auto and marine parts and machine shop operated by Mellon and Moran. The east or river side was adapted to boat repair and the withdrawal of motors from ailing craft. An I-Beam extended over the water and hoisted motors by a chain pull. Wayne County bought out Mellon and Moran and used the building for a garage to store those rugged, chain-drive orange trucks that service Ecorse and the new park. Later the county leased the building to the Ecorse Boat Club.

In the 1940s and beyond, the Ecorse Boat Club members vied for championship titles in shells that they made. A single shell cost approximately $350 in 1940, and it cost about $125 for the club members to build their own shell complete with oars. It took about one hundred hours of labor to complete a single shell composed of four kinds of wood—spruce, mahogany, three-ply ash for ribs and cedar. Most of the club members were factory workers and built and repaired shells and rowed as a hobby.

In January 1940, Coach Charles Tank and Ecorse Township supervisor Bob Brown watched Lawrence Smith put the finishing touches on the

The Ecorse Boat/Rowing Club has consistently produced winning teams and won national competitions.

airplane spruce and mahogany frame of his new racing shell. Ecorse Boat Club members vied for championship honors in shells of their own making during the 1940 rowing season. Any weekday evening in 1940 a visitor could go to the club's boathouse at the foot of Mill Street and Jefferson Avenue and find a score of members busy building new boats and repairing others.

Overcoming mishap and mayhem, the Ecorse Club struggled to glory by winning race after race. Ecorse won Schoolboy Championships, and its lightweight crews won Royal Canadian Henley titles in 1939. In 1940, the first Ecorse High School crew appeared on the Detroit River and reigned as undefeated champions of the metropolitan area at the end of their first season. In 1940, Larry Smith and Pat Messler helped Charles Tank polish the crews that he had guided to championship status by teaching them rowing fundamentals. Even though some of his students did not become members of championship crews, they were the foundation of the Ecorse Rowing Club and passed on what they knew to the next generation of rowers. After Charles Tank died in the spring of 1940, Pat Messler took over as coach of the high school boys, and Larry Smith handled the rest, especially the strong lightweights who consistently defeated Jim Rice's heavyweight Eight from Wyandotte. Messler's boys won the high school Eight race at the Henley. Among those rowing for Ecorse High School were George Pappas, Bill Hughes, Red Alexander, Bob Blair, Bob Vollmer, Earl Neuland, Bob White, Harold Covert, Vic Mitea, Harvey Kromrei, Virgil Ciungan, Reg LeBlanc, Art Bourassa and Harold Marcotte. Larry LeBlanc noted that "even before the renowned Jim Rice came onto the scene, Ecorse Boat Club was a tough, unique group of rowers."

Jim Rice, "The Old Man of the Detroit River"

Jim Rice, close friend of Charles Tank and internationally known rowing coach, became the director of the rowing program at Ecorse in 1942. Rice was born on Hiawatha Island in Lake Ontario off Toronto in 1871 or 1872. He usually waxed vague when asked his age, but when pinned down would tell the story about his father having put down the date in the family Bible as 1872. Hiawatha Island was also the home of Ned Hanlan, probably history's greatest singles sculler, who taught Rice. A tall, strapping man, six feet in his stocking feet, Rice developed early in life the two-fisted manner and the roaring voice that were his trademarks.

Coach Rice brought fifty years of experience coaching championship crews with him to Ecorse. His first coaching job was with the Toronto Rowing Club in 1893, and in 1899 he came to coach the Detroit Boat Club and stayed until 1904, when he accepted an offer from the Weld Boat Club at Harvard. After a two-year stay at Harvard, he transferred to Columbia University, where he served as head coach for seventeen years until 1923. His 1914 Columbia crew won the Poughkeepsie Regatta. In 1927, he returned to the Detroit Boat Club, staying through 1932. The Hamilton Leanders then obtained his services, and he was there for three seasons, returning in 1936 for three more seasons at the Detroit Boat Club. He coached for three years at Wyandotte Boat Club and finally went to the Ecorse Boat Club in 1942, where he stayed until his retirement in 1947. When he agreed to coach the Ecorse Boat Club after the death of his friend Charles Tank, Ecorse and almost every other rowing club in the country recognized him as one of the top-ranking rowing coaches in America.

After he took over as coach in 1942, the Ecorse Boat Club with Rice at its helm was the crew to beat in any race it entered. The Tank brothers, Louis and Red, were still active as scullers and coaches, but the younger men were fast replacing the men who started the club in 1938. The club won many races, and its trophy room was crowded with medals and trophies won in Chicago, Philadelphia and all towns in which rowing was recognized. The Ecorse High School crew won its third straight race in the third annual Down River regatta in August 1941. The winning crew consisted of: George Pappas, stroke; Virgil Ciungan, Harvey Kromrei, Bob White, Reggie LeBlanc, Bob Blair, Earl Newland and Bob Vollmar, bow and front; and Bill Hughes, coxswain. The Tank brothers won the 140-pound doubles and placed second in the heavyweight doubles at the Canadian Henley that year, William Tank won second place in the quarter-mile dash for singles and Louis Tank won second place in the heavyweight singles. The Ecorse High School crew cinched the North American championship at the Henley, and the 140-pound eight also won its race.

The shells that the Ecorse crews used to win their races were so lightweight that crew members almost always had to strive for a precarious balance. Lou Tank, winner of the championship singles in the Down River regatta, collected his medal at the finish line from an improvised basket—a sieve attached to the end of a bamboo pole—because he could not climb out of his shell without capsizing it. He rowed back to a floating dock, and the light shell became unbalanced and capsized.

Crew members Gus Pappas and Irving Kromrei of Ecorse were rowing their way to victory in the high school doubles when Pappas "pulled a crab," which means catching water with an oar while the sculler is recovering or pushing the blades back to dip them in the water. The "crab" knocked their light shell off balance, and it capsized, throwing them into the river. The Ecorse team went on to win, despite the "crab."

The Ecorse "Golden Boys" of 1942 showed their stern to the best boats in the United States. They exceeded hometown expectations when they performed like champions in front of a crowd of twenty-five thousand people lining the Detroit Riverfront in the races of July 4 and 5. Even veteran coach Jim Rice, who usually accepted praise matter-of-factly, glowed with pride at the performance of his oarsmen. Ecorse won practically everything in the regatta, successfully defending their numerous titles and adding more championships to the Ecorse Rowing Club's long list of achievements. Crew members added the Junior Point Trophy, the Senior Point Trophy and the Senior Eight Championship Trophy to the trophy case at the Ecorse Boat Club, as well as various plaques commemorating their Saturday and Sunday victories.

As two of the three remaining members of the original Wah-Wah-Tah-See Club, Alex Beaubien and Elmer Labadie were two of the most interested spectators at the regatta. Alex Beaubien rowed his last singles race in 1889, when he defeated Knight Wright at the Belle Isle races, and he also served as coxswain in the ten-oar barge.

From 1940 to 1942, the Ecorse High School eight lost only one race, rowing at Minneapolis in a borrowed shell set up directly opposite from the one they were familiar with. In 1942, they won both the Junior and Senior Central titles at the Central States Schoolboy regatta in Chicago and both Junior and Senior races at the invitational meet at Culver Military Academy. The 1942 Senior Schoolboy crew also won all major events at the Canadian Henley held at St. Catharines, Ontario, and two eight-oar events within an hour to set a new endurance record. There is no record of any crew ever before winning the Henley heavyweight eight and the high school eight events in a single day. Old-timers who saw the 1942 crew in action voted it one of the best crews in the history of rowing.

Larry LeBlanc recaptured the ambience of rowing on the river in the 1940s and occupying the rowing clubhouse when he recalled cold showers between corrugated walls "while an east wind pushed cold through the sliding doors that faced the river." He remembered the glowing potbellied stove in the clubroom and Jim Rice and other well-toasted oarsmen sitting around it. He remembered "the hub-bub of pool playing, ping pong and the endless stream of creative profanity."

By 1943, most of the "Golden Boys" of 1942 were serving in the armed forces, but Coach Jim Rice felt optimistic about the 1943 crew's performance. The 1943 crew won the Central States Interscholastic championship and went on to win the Canadian Henley. They won six races, were second in one race and third in another to capture all of the major events and finish second in point totals. It was the second year in a row that Ecorse boys under Jim Rice swept the race in the Henley. The 1943 crew also won the High School Eight Championship and the Senior heavyweight, as well. John Whitefield was cox; Harold Marcott, stroke; and John Gregan, Harvey Kromrei, Corky Poppa, Erwin Kromrei, Paul Scott, John Ghinda and Gus Pappas, bow.

The 1942, 1943 and 1944 crews won all events at every regatta they entered, but World War II attrition continued to affect the Ecorse Club. In the spring of 1943 the Ecorse Club regretfully declined the University of Wisconsin invitation to participate in a special spring race including both college and high school crews to be held at the university. Club members felt that "with conditions as they are at present and having lost a number of the members of last years' championship crews to the army and navy the club is unprepared to accept any invitations at this time." During 1944, the Ecorse Boat Club participated in only two regattas because of the war, but they won three first and five seconds in the Henley and the interscholastic championship for the fourth consecutive time. The 1945 Senior crew was: Dallas Lett, Bob Pfeiffer, stroke; Lawrence Pulkownik, John Pulaski, Paul Hanusack, bow; and Richard Emling, Joe Rawson, coxswain. James LeBlanc and Norman Mihatsch went on to win more rowing events.

The *Ecorse Advertiser* announcement of July 2, 1945, lured people to the riverfront by advising:

> *Neither gasoline rationing nor travel restrictions will keep visitors away from Ecorse day for the riverside part is readily accessible by bus from all Metropolitan Detroit. Avoiding the dangers of crowded highways, the discomfort of crowded trains and boats the people of the Metropolitan area may enjoy free of charge the splendid celebration offered by the City of Ecorse.*

The first year that the Ecorse Boat Club held the Oarsmen's Ball was 1938, and by the 1940s, the Ecorse businessmen's association had taken on the job of planning and sponsoring Ecorse Days over the Fourth of July holiday, and in conjunction with the rowing regattas they chose a rowing queen and court. The Boat Club sponsored the Oarsmen's Ball and usually held it at the St. Francis High School auditorium. Elaine MacDonald was crowned rowing queen in July 1942 at the Central States Regatta before the first Saturday afternoon race.

Nellie Muntean was 1945 queen, Donna Schappat won in 1946, twins Clara and Clarice Willis in 1947 and Donna Lewerenz in 1948.

In 1946, the first year of peace with the return of many men from the armed forces, there was a revival of rowing all over the country, and Ecorse Boat Club with Jim Rice coaching came into its biggest season. In 1946, officials included Vernon (Mike) Tank, president; Edward Kromrei, vice-president; Albert Warner, treasurer; Arthur Sims, secretary; and Jim Rice, coach. Rice had two teams competing that year. He selected Mike Stanovich, Bill Smith, Bob Hanusack, Dick Emling, Wayne Dupuis, Norman Mihatsch, Dallas Lett, Larry Pulkownik and Jimmy Osborn as the Ecorse High Varsity Eight to compete. The Ecorse Heavyweight Eight had already won the heavyweight event at the Shriner's Regatta two weeks earler and were practicing for the Central States Rowing Association Regatta on July 4 to compete for honors in their class. On this team were Bob Vollmar, Harold

The Ecorse Rowing Club's Future

During the 1930s, 1940s and 1950s, the Ecorse Boat Club sponsored the Oarsmen's Ball and elected a rowing queen and court.

Covert, Walt Pooley, John Hill, Gus Pappas, Cam Wery, Bob White, George Pappas and John Whitefield.

Mayor Voisine's Two-Week Dream Campaign

As well as Coach Mike Tank, a man named Bill had big plans for the Ecorse Boat Club in 1946. The rowing bug bit Bill Voisine four years earlier, and his conversion to the sport was important for Ecorse oarsman and Ecorse itself. Bill was more formally known as Mayor William F. Voisine, mayor of Ecorse by avocation and head of a prosperous steel company by vocation. The Ecorse Rowing Club was hosting the Central States Associations annual rowing regatta on the Detroit River on July 3 and 4, and Mayor Voisine recognized the possibilities for Ecorse. With the enthusiastic support of Ecorse Boat Club president Mike Tank, the mayor acted. His first step was to improve the club's facilities. He headed a drive that raised $4,000 in one night to purchase a Quonset hut for a boat shed. His chief concern was to make the regatta attractive for spectators, and with that goal in mind he combed the Down River communities for bleachers. He wanted to obtain five thousand free seats for the races.

Mayor Voisine's vision stretched far beyond the 1947 Central States Regatta to making Ecorse the American capital of rowing. He said: "We have everything here. An ideal stretch of water that is largely wind shielded, real public spirit and a wealth of rugged young men who, now the war is over, will make Ecorse oarsmen respected all over the country."

In spring 1946, Mayor Voisine announced a successful two-week campaign to raise funds for a new building for the Ecorse Boat Club to store all of its rowing shells and equipment. He announced the beginning of construction and promised that the building would be ready by the Central States Regatta in July.

As the first step in his campaign, Mayor Voisine appealed to George R. Fink, president of the Great Lakes Steel Corporation. Fink agreed to donate a sixty- by seventy-foot Quonset building. The mayor discovered that federal permission was necessary to erect the building, so he conferred with federal officials in Detroit and Washington. Next, he raised $4,000 for the foundation and construction of the building, including a brick front to match the front of the existing building.

In an *Ecorse Advertiser* story, the mayor detailed a list of Ecorse businesses and individual citizens contributing to the new clubhouse for the Ecorse Rowing Club, including National Steel and the Ecorse Kiwanis Club. The club planned for the new building to be used exclusively to store equipment.

He concluded his story for the *Advertiser* by saying, "It is my desire to provide and do everything within my power to further recreation facilities for Ecorse."

Mayor Voisine's Dream Teams

Mike Tank was reelected to head Ecorse Boat Club for the 1946 season at the annual election of the oarsmen in the main clubroom at West Jefferson and Mill Street. Tank had been president of the local rowing club for several years and guided the club into one of the best contenders in the country. Edward Kromrei was reelected vice-president, an office he, too, had held for several years. The club members reelected Art Sims, Ecorse businessman, as secretary and William Jones, affiliated with the Ecorse-Lincoln Park Bank, as treasurer, a first term for him. The club officials considered their most important task to be completing plans for the ninth annual Oarsmen's Ball, slated for Saturday, February 15, 1947, in the St. Francis High School auditorium.

The Ecorse Rowing Club's Future

Louis Tank, United States and international sculling champion since 1936, was appointed head coach for Ecorse Boat Club crews for the 1947 season. Club officials searched for a suitable coach to replace Jim Rice, who retired from coaching that year, and the name of Louis Tank shone above any other candidates. Tank had been an active oarsman since the Ecorse Boat Club had reorganized in 1938–39, and his achievements had been numerous and consistent in both national and international regattas. With this appointment, he followed in the footsteps of his father, the late Charles Tank, who was first coach of the present club.

Club members expressed deep regret at the retirement of Jim Rice. The *Oarsmen's News* summarized Rice's career in Ecorse when it said that Rice had come to Ecorse in the spring of 1942 and enjoyed much success with Ecorse crews. His schoolboy crews won many championships during 1942–44, and he was very successful with other boat club crews during that time. His record during 1945 was outstanding, and during the 1946 season, Rice's crews were among the best in the United States.

In 1947, the Ecorse crews brought honors to Ecorse by winning the thirty-fourth annual Central States Rowing Regatta held on July 3 and 4 in Ecorse,

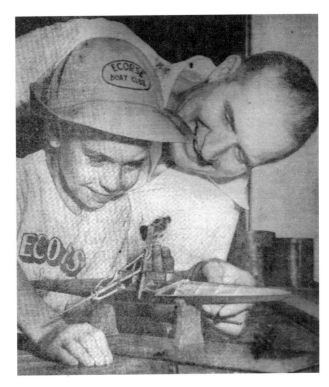

Mayor William Voisine and a young Charles Tank, a member of the famous Tank rowing family. Charles was one of the Ecorse soldiers later killed in Vietnam.

beating their closest rival, the Detroit Boat Club, by more than two hundred points. The only crew to win both a Junior and Senior event was the Ecorse Boat Club's 145-pounds four with coxswain. In the Junior event, the winning oarsmen were Wayne Dupuis, Robert Short, Ed Lett and Bill Wilson, who pulled away from the Chicago, Wyandotte and St. Louis clubs to win in seven minutes, sixteen seconds, just nosing out Wyandotte by a very small margin. Charles Piros, Ecorse High School sculler, pulled to an easy ten-length victory in the high school singles event. The next day he came back in the Senior events with a second-place finish in the 145-pound singles.

Jim Rice invited a famous friend to Ecorse in July 1947. Bob Pearce, world champion professional sculler, was a special guest at the Central States Regatta on Saturday, July 4, and Sunday, July 5. Pearce and Jim Rice were close friends, and Pearce accepted Rice's invitation to attend the regatta.

An Australian by birth, Pearce had held the world title since 1932 and found it increasingly difficult to get competition. He planned to give an exhibition during the regatta. He was the coach at the Leander Boat Club in Hamilton, Ontario, and was recognized as among the best in coaching, as well as sculling.

Grace Kelly's Brother

The *Ecorse Advertiser* of April 1947 carried a discrete headline announcing that an Olympic contender was to train in Ecorse. The story explained that Mr. Jack Kelly of Philadelphia, Pennsylvania, had recently qualified to represent the United States in the 1948 Summer Olympics. He planned to train in the spring and summer of 1947 with members of the Ecorse Boat Club, rowing as a singles sculler, and he would live in Ecorse while he trained. "We wish him well," the *Advertiser* story concluded.

Marvin Graves, a resident of Ecorse at the time, remembers Jack Kelly's time in Ecorse. He said that Jack Kelly quickly got to know Ecorse residents, and he would join the other oarsmen in their morning and evening workouts. He would also jog at least three times a day for miles up and down Jefferson Avenue, the main street in Ecorse. As he jogged by, residents would speak and wave to him, and he always waved back. Some people passing in their cars would honk a greeting at him, and he would smile and wave back.

When he was fourteen years old, Graves worked at Loveland's Drugstore, and Jack Kelly would stop in a few times a day for refreshment at the soda fountain. He remembers Jack Kelly as a pleasant and courteous person.

The Ecorse Rowing Club's Future

Marvin had to sweep the floor as one of his daily duties, and when Marvin swept near Jack Kelly, he would always smile and move his feet or move to another place at the counter without any hard feelings. Everyone working at Loveland's soon began calling him Jack. One summer day, Jack came into Lovelands with a very beautiful girl. He introduced her to the people working there as his sister Pat, who had come for a visit all the way from Philly. It wasn't until sometime later that Marvin realized that her middle name was Patricia and that her first name was Grace. Grace Kelly was his sister! In 1947, she was not yet a celebrity. Her stage debut was in 1949, and her first picture, *Fourteen Hours*, was released in 1951. *High Noon*, her second picture, was released in 1952, the year Marvin graduated from Ecorse High School.

Graves concluded, "There at the soda fountain in Loveland's Drugstore, Ecorse, Michigan, U.S.A., broom in hand, I stood face to face with Grace Kelly and didn't know it!"

The Ecorse Rowing Club's Next Fifty Years

The Ecorse Boat Club's Senior heavyweight eight scored the big victory of the regatta featuring the top-notch prep rollers and scullers of the Midwest, upsetting highly rated Allen Park by two lengths in the feature race. Allen Park's crew had been favored because of a win over the Ecorse rowers a week before in Chicago.

In the spring of 1956, Camille Wery, thirty-one-year-old former rower and Ecorse Rowing Club vice-president, was elected president, succeeding Joe Rawson of Allen Park. Wery had been a Boat Club member since 1942 and was an army veteran. He worked at Great Lakes Steel Corporation and lived with his wife, Jean, and four children in Ecorse Township. Other officers named in the recent election were Fergus Judge, vice-president; Wayne Dupuis, treasurer; and Art Sims, secretary. Bob Short, club spokesman, said that Ecorse would be the host of the 1956 Central States Rowing Association's annual regatta scheduled for July 4 on the Detroit River. The Ecorse Club also was making an all-out effort to qualify crews for the Olympic rowing trials set for June 28 at Syracuse, New York. Ecorse crews were planning to compete against Detroit Boat Club members for the right to represent the Greater Detroit area at the trials, Short said. He added that several Ecorse Boat Club members currently in the service had applied for transfers to the Detroit area so they could begin training for the Olympic trials.

Milton Montie (left) and Art Sims (middle) were active promoters and members of the Ecorse Boat Club.

Community support helped finance the numerous boat club crews and their equipment, and every year the young men in the Ecorse Boat Club would take part in fundraising activities to finance their seasons. On a Tuesday night in early July 1962, the young men of the Ecorse Boat Club canvassed the city between the hours of 6:00 and 9:00 p.m. They offered for sale a decal with the Ecorse Boat Club emblem of crossed oars called "Blades." Spokesman Dave Loveland explained that it was expensive to transport crews and equipment to regattas, where the crews competed against national and international crews. The crews did well in 1962. On July 4 the Ecorse Boat Club crews won their own Water Festival Regatta, rowing against crews from the Detroit Boat Club, Wyandotte, Roosevelt and Chicago. Ecorse emerged victorious in both heavyweight and 135-pound eights and fours and tied with the Detroit Boat Club in the quarter-mile dash. The Detroiters, Ecorse Boat Club's arch rivals, won their sculling specialties—light and heavy singles, open doubles and the quarter-mile single dash. The weekend before, the Ecorse Boat Club sent its Junior crews to London, Ontario, for the Central Ontario Rowing Association Regatta. There they won two races in good competition and placed second in two others by close margins. They were pitted against crews from Wyandotte, Hamilton Leanders, Toronto Dons Rowing Club, St. Catharines and London Rowing Club. Ecorse Boat Club emerged victorious in the 135-pound fours. Ecorse rowers were Jim Montie, Dick Thorburn, Sam Pappas and Bob Burkhardt. Jim Judge, Wayne Berger, Bill Nantau and Karl Schwartz won the heavy fours without a coxswain, even though they had never before rowed together as a unit. Ecorse took seconds in the 135-pound weights and Junior heavyweights, the latter by half a boat length.

Robert Walker Coached the Team

In mid-July 1962, the Ecorse Boat Club's Intermediate eight crew made ready for a trip to the National Association of Amateur Oarsman Regatta, which was held in the Black Rock Channel, Buffalo, New York. The eight earned the trip after a fine showing the week before in a match race with the Detroit Boat Club's crew. The Ecorse contingent lost, but by less than a boat length, leading coach Robert Walker to believe that they could possibly win the Nationals. Members making the trip included Mark Poremba, John Kurtz, Tom Judge, Wayne Burger, Jim Judge, Karl Schwartz and Dave Horvath, accompanied by Coach Robert Walker and Harry Miller.

The Ecorse Boat Club's Intermediate eight crew beat the Detroit Boat Club in a preliminary heat at the National Rowing Regatta in Buffalo and then went on to place second in the finals of the event. Both the Ecorse oarsmen and the winning St. Catharines eight broke records in the race on a two-thousand-meter Olympic course. St. Catharines Club clocked 5:58.8

for the distance, while Ecorse was timed at 6:02. The old record for the course set in 1909 was 6:03.

Ecorse also scored second in the Senior Heavyweight Four without a coxswain, coming in behind a sharp Lake Washington crew. Still farther back was the highly touted four of the Vespers Club of Philadelphia.

According to the club spokesman and later president Dave Loveland, Ecorse racked up a total of twenty-eight points to place seventh overall in the regatta, a creditable showing in the Nationals, which attracted the finest crews from the United States and Canada. The Detroit Boat Club was the overall winner. The Ecorse Club had nine entries in the Canadian Royal Henley Regatta, and Coach Walker felt that his oarsman would be "contenders in every race."

The 1964 Ecorse Boat Club brought home the winning trophy for the Senior 145-pound Four-without-Cox at the Canadian Henley races, which were held on July 25 and televised on August 1. The winning crew was Richard Thorburn, Stroke; Sam Pappas, Three-Man; Robert Burkhardt,

Chefs Gene Maurice, Ari Drouillard, Sharkey Montie and Tom Drouillard used secret, jealously guarded recipes for cooking muskrat, the traditional fundraising treat of St. Anne Rosary Altar Society at St. Francis Church. Down River restaurants also served muskrat dinners.

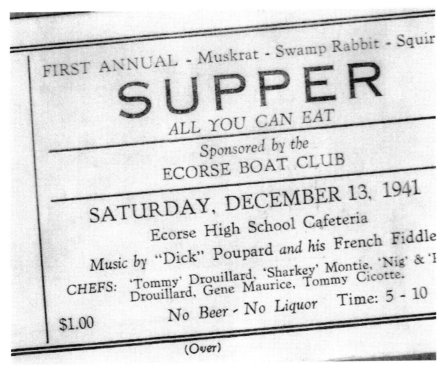

FIRST ANNUAL - Muskrat - Swamp Rabbit - Squir
SUPPER
ALL YOU CAN EAT

Sponsored by the
ECORSE BOAT CLUB

SATURDAY, DECEMBER 13, 1941

Ecorse High School Cafeteria

Music by "Dick" Poupard and his French Fiddle

CHEFS: 'Tommy' Drouillard, 'Sharkey' Montie, 'Nig' & 'I
Drouillard, Gene Maurice, Tommy Cicotte.

$1.00   No Beer - No Liquor   Time: 5 - 10

(Over)

A ticket for the First Annual Muskrat Supper of the Ecorse Rowing Club.

Two-Man; and James Montie, Bow Man. Nick Pappas was the coach and David Loveland club president.

As the Ecorse Boat Club sculled through the '60s, there were still charter members and their descendants from the early days of the club among the membership. One of these members, Larry LeBlanc, wrote his perspective of the club and its coaches in a 1964 column discussing the Rowing Club's second incarnation. He wrote that the Ecorse Boat Club began in 1937–38 when Louise and William "Red" Tank were sculling for the Wyandotte Club, virtually ignoring the first half-century of the club's existence. Then he adds some fascinating inside information about the club and its coaches. According to LeBlanc, along with Charles Tank, Wyandotte coach Lee McClenahan coached the Tank boys to rowing excellence, and while they rowed for Wyandotte, Louie and Red Tank scored over a dozen victories in the scull events in both the United States and Canada.

In 1965, the coaching staff was Louis Hawkings, assistant; Nick Pappas, head coach; and Harry Miller, assistant. Vernon "Mike" Tank was the president of the Ecorse Boat Club from 1938–50. His contemporaries say that "he drank a bottle of beer with a flair that is memorable if not legendary," but when he worked at the Rowing Club he toiled. He cleaned corners, crevices and places where no one else looked. He cleaned thoroughly and cheerfully as part of his presidential duties, and revealing his true character, he cleaned where it didn't show.

Women continued to come into their own in the Ecorse Rowing Club and in the larger world in the 1970s and helped their male counterparts continue Ecorse's winning tradition. In May 1975, the girls' crew of the Ecorse Rowing Club rowed to a solid victory over a girls' crew from London, Ontario. The Ecorse girls traveled to London, where they rowed the four-oared race on the meandering Thames River course. Members of the victorious girls' crew were Janine Morguet, Karen Hawkins, Mary Jane Hric, Debbie Comerzan and Rose Sanflippo, cox. This was the only women's race held.

There were also exhibition races in which the Ecorse boys' crew was victorious in four out of seven races. The girls' crew and the Ecorse High Rowing Team planned to complete the weekend at the Canadian Schoolboy Championships in St. Catharines, Ontario. In a scrimmage race the day before, the girls defeated the Detroit Boat Club girls' crew in the two events that were rowed, the eight-oared shell and four-oared shell. The girls in the eight were Denise Comerzan, Patty Lindel, Debbie Garze, Sherri Judge, Jayne Eberts, Mary Ellen Sizek, Marsha Hawkins, Kim Miller and Shevawn

Rowing is not all serious business.

The Ecorse Rowing Club's Future

Rowing is often a family affair.

Enright, cox. Victorious Ecorse Four were Janet Scesney, Cindy Bair, Debbie Garza, Mary Ellen Sitek and Kathy Schrock, cox.

Councilman Kenneth Slifka, Al Ruthven, Pete Vukovich, Councilman Nike Pappas, Cam Wery and Jack LeBlanc presided over a ceremony in September 1976 to dedicate a four-man scull to Jim Rice. The dedication was part of the Ecorse Rowing Club's Old Timer's Regatta held at the riverfront in September 1976.

In June 1987, the Ecorse Rowing Club appointed a new head coach, Ricky Pollack, from Philadelphia, who had an extensive rowing background and coaching experience. Having first rowed at Undine Barge Club and Vesper for eight years, he went on to various coaching positions at Philadelphia Barge Club, Clark and Worchester Barge Club and Mount Holyoke Rowing Club. He led the Women's Junior National Team in 1980 and Senior B Crew in 1982. Pollack said that he saw a lot of promising potential in the high school boys' crew currently rowing at the club from Carlson. "In another year or two, many will be ready for national competition. They are the future of the club, and we should do our part to make sure that they are successful." Pollack also planned to try to gain support from the community because community support through the years helped to make Ecorse a national rowing stronghold.

Vessels of all kinds use the Detroit River for commerce, competition and recreation.

Knowing which way to row is an important skill.

The 1987 season was the second that Carlson High School team had been based at Ecorse Rowing Club, and although the school had just recently added rowing to the sports that it offered, the average turnout was close to ninety boys and girls. Head coach Ron Lammers worked to prepare the squad for competing in high school regattas across the United States and Canada.

The Ecorse Rowing Club's Future

Most of the boys and girls also rowed for the Ecorse Rowing Club. Girls' novice and varsity lightweight coaches Mary Ann Van Boxell and Beth Ann Gretka expected most of their girls to return to row in the summer as well. It had been many years since women rowed at Ecorse, and this added new dimension to the Ecorse Boat Club.

In 1990, a women's crew, the Argonaut crew, convincingly won the Ecorse Rowing Club Arthur Sims Memorial Trophy, and the Argonaut crew won the Intermediate Women's 125-pound eight event at the 1990 Royal Canadian Henley Regatta. This was the first year that the Arthur Sims Memorial Trophy was presented, and Robert Sims, Arthur's son, and Ecorse Rowing Club board member Joe Rawson presented the trophy.

During the last two decades of the twentieth century and into the twenty-first century, the Ecorse Rowing Club has continued its 135-year tradition of winning crews. Ecorse Rowing Club has provided a source of community pride and recreation for 135 years and will continue to do so.

CHAPTER 8

ELI LEBLANC WITNESSES RUMRUNNING IN ECORSE

The *Detroit Evening News* recorded an instance in which the Detroit River helped sober someone up, the exact opposite of what happened on the river in the rumrunning days of the 1920s and 1930s. The *Evening News* reported that Albert Latour was soused in the river yesterday off Belle Island, and it sobered him right off. When nearby boaters picked him up, he said that he had "shadows flitting around him." The only shadow his rescuers found was a whiskey bottle nearly emptied. They picked up him and his skiff and took them to Belle Island.

During the 1920s and 1930s, the Ecorse waterfront, especially near Jefferson and Southfield and a strip of riverfront called Hogan's Alley, became notorious for its nightclubs. Gambling, bootlegging and other nefarious activities took place on the Ecorse waterfront, and bandits and gamblers from Detroit routinely traveled to Ecorse to ply their trades and hide out from the police. In 1920, Albert M. Jaeger had become the first salaried fire chief in Ecorse and, with a force of three men, took up office in the wooden city hall across from his house. At age fifty-seven in 1945, he went to his office at the fire department in the new municipal building to receive the hearty congratulations of the twenty-eight-member fire department.

About 1922, two years after he was installed as Ecorse's first fire chief, Village President Fred Bouchard made Jaeger acting chief of police. He held the two offices jointly until 1926, and this provided material for local jokesters. The story had it that Jaeger always worked bareheaded in his office until a call came demanding his services as one department head or another. Then he would grab the correct hat, jam it on his head and run out of his office to whatever challenge lay ahead.

Holding the joint office was difficult in the turbulent days of bootlegging and rumrunning in Ecorse. Several underworld hideouts had sprung up along the riverfront, huddled beside the river below Southfield Road. One of them was known as "Robbers Roost" and often sheltered notorious lawbreakers. One March day in 1924, Jaeger and one of his men, Benjamin Montie, a fire truck driver and auxiliary policemen, went down to Robber's Roost to investigate a case of petty larceny. Inside, two bandits who had just raided the Commonwealth Bank in Detroit and escaped with $17,000 were counting their money. Chief Jaeger and Benjamin Montie took the men to police headquarters for questioning, and then Jaeger, Montie and two deputy sheriffs returned to Robber's Roost, where they found two more of the bandit ring in hiding.

The two men jumped out of a window into the river. They swam back to shore and were captured just as two others drove up in a car. They were Bernard Malley, Leo Corbett, Eliza Meade and Tim Murray. Meade and Corbett were in the car, and Corbett drew a gun and killed Ecorse patrolman-fireman Benjamin Montie. Then Chief of Police Jaeger drew his gun and killed Corbett.

During the scuffle, Meade drove away in the car, and a statewide hunt failed to find him. (Later he was arrested in Arizona and sentenced to twenty to forty years in Marquette Prison.) As the bank robbers attempted to get away, they threw the $17,000 over the streets and waterfront. Spectators did not return their spoils.

Following the family tradition, Eli "Peck" LeBlanc's generation played an important part in Ecorse history. In a 1966 interview with Ecorse native JoAnn Coman, he recalled Prohibition days. According to Eli, Mud Island, which was formed by logs from a nearby sawmill, acted as a screen for an important tunnel constructed by smugglers. This tunnel extended about two blocks inland and was made in such a manner as to allow the boat to travel on the water and still remain below ground. The rumrunners then unloaded the liquor in a combination garage/gambling house on Monroe Street.

LeBlanc vividly recalled Hogan's Alley in Ecorse, a small side street composed of a row of dimly lit shacks sometimes used as private bars that were called "blind pigs." The majority of liquor runs ended at Hogan's Alley, but only smugglers and select guests who knew the password were admitted to Hogan's Alley. Once inside, sights to be enjoyed included young men wearing fancy clothes and diamond rings in imitation of Al Capone, piles of money changing hands and countless cocktails disappearing down thirsty throats. Some people called Hogan's Alley the toughest territory in the country during Prohibition times.

In continuous stories, Detroit newspapers investigated the Prohibition years in Ecorse. Charles Creinn of the *Detroit Times* said that Ecorse, formerly

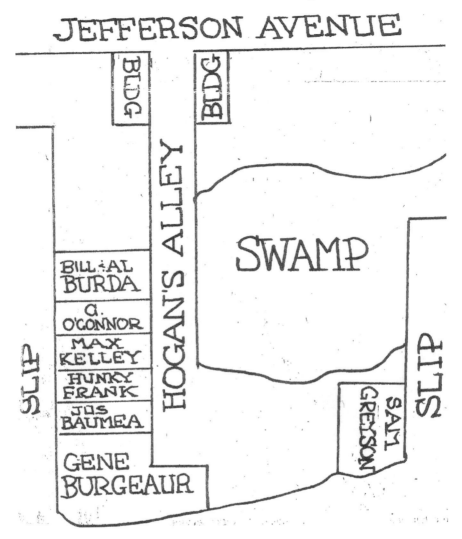

Hogan's Alley, shown on this map, was a bootlegging hotspot during Prohibition.

a small, peaceful resort area, became a notorious "rum row" and the center of a dangerous and risky but profitable industry after national Prohibition was passed in 1920. According to Creinn, millions of dollars changed hands at one time in Ecorse, and the three banks in the village of less than ten thousand inhabitants did a thriving business. People made fortunes overnight and lost them just as quickly.

Orval L. Girard of the *Detroit Times* reminisced with one foot propped on a weather-beaten pier on Southfield Dock. "There was nothing but a swamp where the steelworks stand. All along the river front customs picket boats cruised day and night in hopes of discovering the rumrunning operations in Canada."

The *Wyandotte Herald* joined the story parade but said that bootleggers let Ecorse citizens go in peace unless they interfered with snuggling operations. "For a number of years following the advent of Volsteadism, 90 percent of the beer and strong liquor reaching Michigan from Canada came by way of Ecorse," said the *Herald*. Before Prohibition, a few boathouses and cottages along the river front were used for legitimate purposes, it concluded.

Then, during 1918, boathouses once sheltering pleasure craft were converted to storage for liquor and luggers, which were high-speed boats that transported goods across the river. Summer cottages were turned into gambling houses with a variety of entertainment. Most of these changes were made along a half-mile stretch of land not more than a city block wide.

Another *Detroit News* reporter, Martha Torplitz, wrote that Ecorse changed its personality at night because a Canadian regulation required rum boats to be clear of the piers before nightfall. These boats could travel to Canada at random and load and leave when they pleased as long as they were finished before sundown. The fleet would drop down the foreign side of the Detroit River and await a chance to escape. Sunset shook the fleet from its daytime drowsiness. Trained eyes watched for signals. A red and green lantern indicated "departure an hour from now," while two red ones meant "start at once."

Often more than fifty boats—from fifty footers to flat busses, smaller power boats, rowboats and skiffs—waited to escape to Ecorse shores. The escape required skillful navigating because the boats did not have lights, and the skippers did not always know who was friend or foe. Sometimes prohibition agents' boats disguised themselves as rumrunner and rumrunners often turned into prohibition agents for an evening. A skipper had to have keenly attuned senses to be able to tell friend from foe on the river after dark.

As soon as a boat touched the dock, hired men began loading the liquor into trucks and cars, a job that required timing, organization and craftiness. Some bootleggers tied cases of beer under the floorboards of trucks and cars and installed liquor-holding trays under dashboards and hoods. Their padded interior prevented the bottles from breaking even during the roughest chases and during the washboard ride over highways to Detroit, Toledo and Chicago. Some wrapped bottles in burlap and hung them from the bottoms of boats for the ride to market, and a few enterprising others installed trays below boxcars on trains and then wired the numbers of their cars to the buyers waiting at the train's destination.

Eli LeBlanc Witnesses Rumrunning in Ecorse

Eli "Peck" LeBlanc picked up the narrative again when he said that cash was the only exchange in this crude bootlegging business with extraordinarily high stakes. As long as the Ecorse rumrunners were paid, they did not worry about a load being hijacked, lost or misdirected. But if a customer did not pay cash on delivery, the consequences could be cold-blooded murder. Or if someone put false labels on the merchandise to get a higher price for cheap liquor and their customers discovered the trick, the deal could end in a rain of bullets. Police and civilians alike routinely fished bullet-riddled bodies out of the Detroit River.

According to LeBlanc, policemen were not always on the right side of the law. Sometimes official eyes were encouraged not to see the bootlegging activities, and sometimes the law ignored the bootleggers out of fear for their lives. "It was common knowledge that police officers were bribed and paid off in other ways to keep quiet."

Ecorse stood wide open for liquor activities other than transferring it. Ecorse was safe for a night on the town. Ladies in evening dresses kicked up their respectable heels on Jefferson Avenue or did the Varsity Drag in buildings that witnessed more decorous activities during the day. If shots punctuated the hours of an evening out, no one looked up from his drink, for shots were ordinary sounds in Ecorse. Anyone could go down Jefferson Avenue day or night to visit roadhouses like the White Tree, Marty Kennedys, the Riverview and Tom R. _____, run by a former policemen. Many people knew Patsy Lowrey's on Eighth Street with the back room decorated in western style with sawdust on the floor and a tin-voiced piano echoing through the room. The price across the bar was fifty cents for whiskey and twenty-five cents for beer.

Dr. Arthur Payette, another Ecorse pioneer, practiced dentistry in Ecorse for thirty-five years in his office overlooking Hogan's Alley and pointed out a different side of bootlegging in Ecorse. Some ordinary citizens as well as professional bootleggers wanted to get rich quick, and with the right connections, packaged ingredients for making beer could be acquired for nominal fees. Stills and other needed apparatus could be found in basements of houses concentrated on Goodell Street, and some "home breweries" specialized in watering liquor by inserting a syringe through the cork of the bottle, extracting the liquor and replacing it with water.

Dr. Payette said that for several years the government did not make much of an effort to stop Canadian liquor from coming into the United States, and when it did try to enforce the law, the rumrunners usually won out. The rumrunners would pay any price for a speedboat if it was fast enough to outrun the law. Some of the customers used to complain bitterly about the prices when protection had to be split five ways: local, federal, state, county and customs. He vividly recalled a state trooper who came to his office for a teeth cleaning. According to Dr. Payette, State Trooper G_____ was already out to get Ecorse, and during the teeth cleaning he managed to work in some comments about the interesting view of Hogan's Alley and the bootlegging activity in Ecorse. Dr. Payette silently continued cleaning the state trooper's teeth. "Minding one's own business was the best policy," the doctor said.

The *Detroit News* continued to publish stories detailing bootlegging operations in "Wild West" Ecorse. Journalist F.L. Smith wrote in the *Detroit News* that

> *to have seen Ecorse in its palmy days is an unforgettable experience, for no gold camp of the old west presented a more glamorous spectacle. It was a perpetual carnival of drinking, gambling, and assorted vices by night and a frenzied business-like community by day. Silk-shirted bootleggers walked its streets and it was the Mecca for the greedy, the unscrupulous, and the criminal of both sexes. When the police desired to lay their hands on a particularly hard customer, they immediately looked in Ecorse and there they generally found him.*

The "perpetual carnival" began on August 11, 1921, when shipments of beer and liquor from Canada to the United States became unlawful. This opened up a glittering world of rumrunning, roustabouts and riches for the ordinary people of Ecorse. Three Ecorse workers immediately took their savings and traveled to Montreal, where the sale of liquor was legal. They bought twenty-five cases of whiskey and drove back to Windsor. Over and over they rowed a small boat back and forth across the river until all of their treasure was ferried to the American side. They posted a lookout for Canadian and American customs officials just in case, but all went well. They sold their liquor in Ecorse and used their profits to finance a second and third trip. Multiply this enterprise by the thousands, and you have some idea of the volume of rumrunning across the river. Both Canadians and Americans with their secret caches of beer and liquor waited "like Indians" among the trees and tall grasses on the Canadian side of the river. Boatloads of smugglers would glide across the river, signaling with pocket torches. A blue light flashed once and then twice—"all was clear." A large sheet hung on a clothesline meant "turn back immediately, police arrived."

Rumrunning boats by the dozens were moored each day at the Ecorse municipal dock at the foot of State Street (now Southfield), which ran through the village's central business district. Rumrunners transferred their cargos to waiting cars and trucks, while residents, police and officials watched. Officials erected a board fence to protect the waterfront, but rumrunners went around or beneath it. Some Canadian breweries set up export docks on the shore just outside of LaSalle, Ontario, which is directly across the Detroit River from Ecorse. Fighting Island, situated in the middle of the river between Ecorse and LaSalle, conveniently hid rumrunners from police patrols.

Rumrunning didn't discriminate in Ecorse. Ecorse rumrunners employed as many as twenty-five schoolboys as spies, lookouts and messengers. In 1922, police arrested a fifteen-year-old boy delivering a truckload of liquor to a Down River roadhouse. The boy said that he was only one of several local boys working for the rumrunners. He insisted that he worked only on weekends and nights so he would not miss school. These thirteen- to sixteen-year-old boys made such good lookouts that the police could not make unannounced raids on blind pigs and boathouse storage centers in Ecorse. The lookout boys usually spotted the police long before they arrived. One state police officer complained that "they spread out along the waterfront and are very awake and diligent."

Federal and state officials also had a difficult time making rumrunning arrests stick in Ecorse because the local police were in sympathy, if not cahoots, with the rumrunners. Rumrunners served on juries, and the only cases from Ecorse tried successfully were the ones tried in federal courts.

Another Wild West–style battle between law and order and the rumrunners and their defenders took place in 1928 in Hogan's Alley. Several cars and three boats holding about thirty customs border patrol inspectors gathered at the end of Hogan's Alley at the foot of State Street (Southfield) to wait in ambush for the rumrunners. Rumrunning boats pulled up to a nearby pier, and the agents rushed them and arrested the seven crew members.

As soon as they were arrested, the crew of the boat yelled for help. Rescuers rushed from all around. Over two hundred people arrived to stop the agents from leaving with the prisoners. The people attacked the customs agents' cars. They slashed tires and broke windshields. They pushed other cars across the alley entrance and threw rocks and bottles at the agents. Before the situation became too desperate, the agents banded together, rushed the barricade and escaped.

John Wozniak of Ecorse is remembered as one of the more honest rumrunners. Wozniak's early twenties coincided with the early rumrunning years in Ecorse. He was enterprising enough to form his own navy of twenty-five "sailors" to carry Canadian liquor into America across the

Detroit River. Wozniak gave his sailors standing orders to avoid violence. Wozniak's men did not carry arms and neither did he. When one of his men got caught, Wozniak backed him and his defense and paid the fine if the rumrunner was convicted.

His love of sports ended John Wozniak's empire. He sponsored a football team, and his team became well known in Ecorse, Lincoln Park, Wyandotte and River Rouge. Law enforcement people would come to the games, frequently to identify the rumrunners on Wozniak's team. In 1928, federal law enforcement officials broke up a large bribery ring, and with his protection gone, Wozniak was arrested. At his trial, Wozniak told the judge, "When I was indicted I was through for good. The law was getting too strong. I sold my boats and scuttled the others. I went into the automobile business and have done pretty well."

In the early rumrunning days, the atmosphere on the river resembled a twenty-four-hour party. Women participated with men in the bootlegging, and the person in the next boat could be a local councilman or the school drama teacher. Boat owners could transport as many as 2,500 cases of liquor each month at a net profit of $25,000 with the owner earning about $10,000. Some rumrunners made 800 percent profit on a load of liquor. The only real perils of the sea that the rumrunners encountered during those first years were losing directions in the middle of the river at night and collisions with other boats.

In the winter, the river often froze solid, and the rumrunners took advantage of the ice road. They used iceboats, sleds and cars to transport liquor from the Canadian side to Ecorse. Convoys of cars from Canada crossed the ice daily. Cars on the American shore lined up at night and turned on the headlights to provide an illuminated expressway across the ice. A prolonged cold spell in January and February 1930 produced thick and inviting ice on Upper Lake Erie and the Detroit River. Hundreds of tire tracks marked the ice trail from the Canadian docks to the American shore. On a February morning in 1930, a *Detroit News* reporter counted seventy-five cars leaving the Amherstburg beer docks. He wrote that ten carried Ohio license plates and headed downriver for south and east points on the Ohio shore. Others drove to the Canadian side of Grosse Ile. When they arrived on Grosse Ile, the liquor was loaded into camouflaged trucks and driven across the toll bridge to the American mainland.

But most of the cars drove from the Amherstburg docks to Bob-Lo Park around the north end of Bob-Lo Island. From there the trail headed west to the Livingston Channel. When the channel was safely reached, the cars drove south for a mile, where the trail forked. One trail led to a slip on the lower end of Grosse Ile, the other led about two miles farther north. As the car drove, the road was about two miles from the upper end of Bob-Lo Park to the Grosse Ile slip. It was about a six-minute ride over the ice.

The dangerous part of the ride was along the Bob-Lo Park side, where the ice was tricky. The rumrunners drove as far as they could with two wheels on the shore. The road from the upper end of Bob-Lo Island to Grosse Ile was safe and the ice solid. The rumrunners did not try to hide their goods from the law. One of them told the *Detroit News* that "the law isn't the thing we fear most. What we are really afraid of is the ice. Anytime it may give way beneath and let one of us through."

The iceboats were the bane of the Coast Guard cutters because they were fast enough to be phantoms for the pursuers. Iceboats had obvious advantages over cars on frozen Lake St. Clair and the Detroit River. Sail-equipped iceboats could speed across the river in twelve minutes or less. Law officers did not have much hope of catching them. The *Detroit News* summed up the situation: "A gust of flying snow and perhaps now and then a trace of silver canvas in the wind and the boats were gone."

Both police and rumrunners used their ice imaginations. Rumrunners nailed ski runners to boats and pushed them across Lake St. Clair or towed several behind a car. When the police got too close, the rumrunners cut their boats loose. The federal agents fit a spiked attachment called ice creepers over their shoes. But running with creepers was slow. Some rumrunners, knowing this, wore ice skates and gracefully skated away.

In 1921, the pirates, including a famous one called the Gray Ghost, moved in. Go-betweens called pullers would carry cash across the river to the Canadian export docks for large purchases. Many of the pullers were robbed and killed and their bodies tossed into the river. In 1922, it was a nightly occurrence to find bodies floating in the river near Ecorse. The Gray Ghost was responsible for a few of these bodies, but generally he remained a gentleman pirate and let his victims escape with their lives. The Gray Ghost was the most famous pirate on the river. His official titles included pirate, extortionist, counterfeiter and friend of the Purple Gang from Detroit. People called him the Gray Ghost because he piloted a gray boat and dressed entirely in gray, including a gray hat and mask. He carried two gray pistols and a gray machine gun. One of his favorite tricks was plundering pullers on the way to Canada. He would intercept them in midstream, using his powerful speedboat to relieve them of their cash.

Once the rumrunners got their liquor across the river from Canada, they could dispose of it in several ways. Some syndicates paid farmers $20,000 or more to store liquor in their barns around Detroit. Others moved in, uninvited, to the docks and storage areas of the wealthy homeowners across the Detroit River and Lake St. Clair. In 1922 alone, at least $35,000 worth of liquor came to Detroit through the seventy miles of river and lakefront stretching from Lake St. Clair to South Rockwood. When the Gray Ghost traveled to Canada for his buying trips, he had a large selection of liquor from which to choose. On the Canadian side of the river, the exporters had rows and rows of liquor docks. They could replenish their stock from eighty-three breweries and twenty-three distilleries.

The Gray Ghost continued pirating without too much interference and disposed of his booty among the bootlegging syndicates of Detroit. Then one day he made a fatal error. He purchased a large load of liquor in Canada with a bad check and irritated some prosperous wholesalers. Five of the wholesalers kicked in $1,000 each and hired someone to eliminate the bad check problem. Rumor had it that the gunman worked for the Purple Gang, but the murder of the Gray Ghost was never solved nor was his true identity ever discovered.

Ecorse continued to suffer a bad reputation throughout all of this rumrunning activity. Delos G. Smith, U.S. district attorney, characterized Ecorse as "one of two black eyes for Detroit." To prove his point he warned Mayor Bouchard that if he did not enforce some law and order within thirty days he would send in the state police. The state police conducted a continuous waterfront vigil, powerful enough to cause most of the smugglers and bootleggers to move their business to Lake St. Clair in the north and Lake Erie in the south. But the liquor smugglers had one power point over the police. They had once used the patrol boat *Alladin* as a rum ship without the police ever knowing it.

It took more than four years of hard work and strategy for the police to capture and convict the bootleggers. When Jefferson Avenue was widened in 1929, the shacks along Hogan's Alley were destroyed, and the city bought the thin strip of land by the waterfront for a park.

Then Prohibition was repealed. A stroke of the pen demolished an entire flourishing industry in December 1933. The rumrunners were legalized out of business, and Ecorse city officials tore down the fence by the waterfront and created a park.

In 1936, the *Ecorse Advertiser* summarized Prohibition and the changing waterfront in Ecorse when it published a lengthy obituary called "Requiem for Walter Locke and Rum Row for Walter Locke," Locke being a waterfront colleague of Eli "Peck" LeBlanc. Walter Locke and his partner Ned Magee owned a boathouse restaurant at the State Street (now Southfield) dock, and from this vantage point they witnessed the scores of men, boys, women and girls creating the Prohibition drama. Locke saw the scattered boathouses on the banks of the river that had been built at the turn of the century for pleasure boating but had been taken over by a generation of people who worked at night and got rich quickly. Rents for the waterfront shacks escalated from $10 a month to $100. He saw smuggling grow in volume and intensity and a class of men rise who gloried in their own skill, strength and acumen at outwitting the people who sought to enforce the Prohibition law.

Time passed, and Locke heard the voices of thirsty Americans demanding whiskey and beer grow louder. He saw the profits for handling them climb higher. The price of cheap whiskey arose to $100 per case—whiskey which would eventually fall back to its norm of $24 or $30 per case.

Bootlegging demographics changed as adventurous youngsters and their outboard motorboats displaced the strong men rowing their sturdy boats across the Detroit River. It took the youngsters and their motorboats ten minutes to cover the distance it took a man one hour and forty minutes to row. Then, as cargos grew bigger, the luggers, with their huge flat-bottomed hulls that could hold hundreds of cases of beer, and sleek, swift speedboats with more costly cargos of whiskey displaced the motorboats.

Walter watched rum row blossoming at night into a sea of colored lights and music. He watched the half-mile south from State Street to Ecorse Creek become a glittering cabaret center that became known as the "Half Mile of Hell." The narrow streets were crowded with automobiles from dusk until dawn, and people surged on foot from one spot to another in a frenzied search for entertainment. They paid fifty cents a bottle for beer and fifty or seventy-five cents for a glass of whiskey. A meal cost them two dollars, and they tipped poor entertainers one dollar and thought they were getting their money's worth.

Walter watched the gambling spots open and thrive in the encouraging atmosphere and witnessed fortunes made and lost on the turn of a wheel or the flip of a card. He saw one poor Ecorse man make $100,000 in a single night and lose $80,000 of it back again within a few days.

Everyone but "the law" thrived. The uphill battle of the law did not change. Walter Locke saw the law, always in clumsier boats than the bootleggers. The outnumbered "Lawmen hung with the tenacity of bulldogs on their quarry," but better equipment and the sheer force of numbers thwarted their best efforts.

Then Walter Locke watched the fall of rum row on the Detroit River in Ecorse. It did not fall as gradually as it had risen; instead rum row shattered like a bottle smashed against a brick wall. He watched the riverfront shacks where millions and millions of dollars' worth of illicit liquor had been stored and passed on become disused and abandoned and then razed to their concrete foundations. He watched the narrow, dirt River Road turn into a broad ribbon of concrete called Jefferson Avenue and then widen yet again, almost to his doors. He watched a growing stream of traffic whiz by and drivers not even glancing at famous local history spots.

Walter and Ned sat on the little veranda of their houseboat restaurant discussing a requiem for rum row. Goodbye to the fortunes lost when the law raided rum row and found the "plant" where the liquor was concealed. Goodbye to the whiskey cars that whipped into and out of the secret boat well garages. Goodbye to the shots ringing out in the night and the lifeless bodies on the river shores of the boys who had "taken the night boat to Buffalo."

Goodbye to the fortunes won in overnight operation and to the desperate chances that were taken with life and liberty to make a "stake." Goodbye to the private operations of the "boys," and hello to the gangsters who muscled in to take the wealthier of the boys on a one-way ride. The jolly fellows who freely spent their money disappeared, and tight-lipped gangsters took their places. The uproarious nature of the waterfront turned into a furtive, stealthy fog. Once or twice a "muscler" offered to cut himself into Walter and Ned's business. Ned would appear the next day with skinned knuckles or maybe his arm in a sling. Nothing else was said or done.

Large-scale bribery ruled the day, and rumrunners and prohibition agents went to jail. Legal exports from Canada stopped, and it became more profitable to make beer on the side. Whiskey was cut, and alky was brewed in alleys by "the Dagoes." Suddenly Ecorse was "dead," and so was Walter Locke. If he had lived until the next summer, Walter would have watched trees spreading leafy branches over the county park along the former Detroit River rum row where so much whiskey had landed at midnight. Flowers swayed in the breeze where once dancers had swayed to cabaret music, and fishermen instead of rumrunners boated on the river. Perhaps, after all, Walter Locke watched and approved.

CHAPTER 9

THE BOB-LO BOATS AND BOB-LO ISLAND

Frank F. Kirby designed the *Columbia*, built in Wyandotte and Detroit in 1902, and the *Ste. Claire*, built in Toledo and launched on May 7, 1910, entering service later that year. The *Ste. Clair* was named after Lake St. Clair and the St. Clair River, and the *Columbia*, named after Christopher Columbus, celebrated its 100th birthday in 2002. It is the oldest steamer in the United States with the exception of ships classed as ferries.

Like all North American steamers, the *Columbia* and *Ste. Claire* are propeller driven. The *Ste. Claire* is 197 feet long, 65 feet wide and 14 feet deep. Its tonnage is 870 gross register tonnage and 507 net register tonnage, and its engine is triple expansion steam with 1,083 horsepower. It can carry 2,500 people, and it served for eighty-one years on a single run—a record unequalled in U.S. maritime history. The *Columbia* is the older of the two Bob-Lo boats. It is 216 feet long overall and was last licensed to carry 2,500 people. The history of the *Columbia* and *Ste. Claire* are intertwined with an island in the Detroit River that generations of twentieth-century people know as Bob-Lo Island.

In the early 1700s, French priests established a Catholic mission on the island for the Huron Indians, and the French christened the island "Bois Blanc" after the beech trees that covered the island—"the Island of white wood." English tongues stumbled over the words Bois Blanc, so they corrupted the name to Bob-Lo until 1949, when the island became officially known as Bob-Lo Island. The island, three miles long and one-half mile wide, is located about eighteen miles downriver from downtown Detroit and is a five-minute ferry ride from Amherstburg, Ontario. In 1796, the British established a military post at Fort Malden in Amherstburg, and thousands of Indians from all tribes journeying to trade furs with the British camped on the island. For a time, Tecumseh, the Shawnee leader, aided the British in

The Bob-Lo Boats *Columbia* and *Ste. Clair* provided enchantment and voyages to Bob-Lo Island on the Detroit River for over fifty years.

the War of 1812 and made Bois Blanc his headquarters, using it as a base to attack the American mainland.

In 1839, a lighthouse was built on the southern side of Bois Blanc to guide ships into the narrow straits behind it. Captain James Hackett was hired as lighthouse keeper and owned 14 acres of the island on a lifetime lease. In the 1850s, Colonel Arthur Rankin, MP, bought the remaining 225 acres of the island from the Canadian government for forty dollars.

During the Civil War, escaping slaves used Bois Blanc Island as a station stop on the Underground Railroad route to Canada. They landed on the beach and rested for a few hours or a few days before continuing their journey to Amherstburg and a new life in Canada.

In 1869, Colonel Rankin sold Bois Blanc to his son, Arthur McKee Rankin, who starred in the New York theatre scene and belonged to New York's fashionable set. He built himself an elaborate estate on the island, stocked the grounds with deer, wild turkey and elk, built extensive stables and treated his New York friends to Bois Blanc hospitality. Eventually, his stage career ended, and he was forced to sell the island to partners Colonel John Atkinson and James A. Randall. Colonel Atkinson's heirs sold the island to what was then the Detroit, Belle Isle and Windsor Ferry Company. In 1898, the Bob-Lo Excursion Line was created, and the island was developed as a resort. In the beginning, Bob-Lo Island promised a day on the Detroit River and a picnic in the pastoral beauty of the island. Henry Ford commissioned Albert Kahan to design a dance hall, which in 1903 was billed as the world's second largest. A carousel provided music and rides.

The boat ride to Bob-Lo contributed greatly to the island's mystique. The boarding dock in Detroit started out at the foot of Woodward Avenue but was moved to the rear of Cobo Hall. The Bob-Lo boat also stopped at Down River communities like Ecorse, Wyandotte and Trenton. The boarding dock eventually moved to Gibraltar in 1981. It took just over an hour to voyage to Bob-Lo Island. Captain Bob-Lo and many bands and other entertainers made the voyage seem as brief as a toot of the Bob-Lo boat whistle. The bands on the second-deck dance floor changed with the times—from Mrs. Walpola's turn-of-the-century music to the 1940s big bands to the Latin Counts of the 1980s.

The Brownings hired Captain Bob-Lo, alias Joe Short, from the Ringling Brothers Circus to entertain the children on the Bob-Lo cruise, and he did just that between 1953 and 1973. He always wore an oversized hat and binoculars and handed out coloring books and small toys to the children on the trips. Captain Bob-Lo retired at the age of ninety. He died in 1975, still singing the praises of Bob-Lo.

There were also moonlight cruises on the Bob-Lo boats. To teenagers and older romantics, the combination of the soft summer breezes, moonlight on the river and that special person alongside made for an unforgettable experience. Often the Bob-Lo boat would just travel down the river to Bob-Lo Island, arrive there about 10:00 p.m. and turn around, but that was enough time for a memorable evening.

The American government made an unprecedented exception for draft-age men during World War I. The law said that draft-age men could not leave the country (Bob-Lo is a Canadian Island), but officials decided that it would be too much of a hardship for young Michigan men to be forbidden to go to Bob-Lo with their sweethearts during the summer. The Great Depression of the 1930s stopped the national economy in its tracks, and the Bob-Lo excursions as well. Then Franklin Delano Roosevelt's 1933 inauguration brought new hope, the New Deal and returning prosperity to the nation. In 1935, the Bob-Lo boats resumed their Detroit River runs.

Financial trouble loomed for the Detroit and Windsor Ferry Company again in 1949. Arthur John Reaume, the mayor of Windsor, suggested that the island be turned into a national park, but the Browning family of Grosse Point, owners of a steamship line, bought the island and the boats. They turned Bob-Lo into an amusement park, building rides, roller coasters and a funhouse. They installed a Ferris wheel, a dance hall and an antique car exhibit. They brought in three hundred exotic animals for a zoo, leading off with Socrates II, a giraffe, and built a mini railroad for rides around the island. In 1961, the Brownings replaced the island landing dock with the deck of the freighter *Queenston*, sunk in place. In 1973, they built the Thunder Bolt roller coaster of steel, and it was one of the largest in the country. Another popular ride was the flue, a log carrying riders down a water slide. In 1975, the Brownings restored the original forty-horse carousel from 1878, and it delighted children and adults alike until it was sold off piece by piece at auction in 1990.

The Brownings sold Bob-Lo Island in 1979, and it passed through the hands of several owners, including the American Automobile Association (AAA) of Michigan. Rowdiness on the boats and on the island in the 1980s caused the crowds to continue diminishing, and when Canadian police and immigration officials spent a day in 1987 rounding up members of the Outlaws motorcycle gang, the end of a ninety-year era drew nearer. In January 1996, the steamers *Columbia* and *Ste. Claire*, which had carried as many as 800,000 visitors to Bob-Lo Island every year in the glory years, were sold at auction. Both steamers need restoration, and efforts are being made to save them and put them back on the Detroit River. The *Columbia* has been designated a National Historical Landmark, the government's premiere designation for historical resources.

CHAPTER 10

ECORSE PEOPLE

Dr. Robert McQuiston's Fifty-Year Office Hours

Dr. Robert McQuiston grew up in the Ecorse of Mayor William Voisine, Dummey's Pool Hall and the old red brick Ecorse Presbyterian Church. Over half a century later, from his office on West Jefferson that sits only a few blocks from his old homesteads on Applegrove and Union Streets, he considered the contours of Ecorse history and how his own life fit into them like a jigsaw puzzle piece. In 2006 he celebrated his fiftieth year of practice in Ecorse. As well as maintaining a private practice and caring for some patients for over fifty years, Dr. McQuiston served as health officer for the Ecorse Police Department.

Born in Ecorse in 1927, the future doctor attended School One and later School Two, and it just took a word or a question to release a memory mobile of some of the smells, sights and sounds of growing up in Ecorse in the late 1930s and 1940s. Shoes are put on as part of our ordinary morning routine, but Dr. Bob remembered more about taking them off as soon as the snow melted off the ground and keeping them off all summer. If his shoes needed to be repaired before school started, he and his mother would take them to the shoemaker on Jefferson to get new heels or whatever else they needed. Shoes can also be taken off for effect, which Bob and his friends did, along with their socks, in the closed-up rooms of the winter school after sledding or walking in the snow. They would put the socks on the radiator and the shoes next to it and wait for the steam to waft the odors of multiple wet socks and shoes throughout the building. "I can still smell them," he says with a twinkle in his eye.

The sights of Ecorse that he saw in his early years that still exist today include the Southfield and Outer Drive Viaducts and the Ecorse waterfront.

The Ecorse Library he remembered in its former location in the old city hall on High Street, before Mayor Voisine led the campaign for a new library on the corner of Outer Drive and Jefferson. "That building had a personality all its own. I liked that building," he said. Another sight he remembered but which later classes might question is Miss Blanche Elliot as a pretty young woman. Ecorse High School students who she taught closer to her 1962 retirement remember her simply as "the Terror of 212," the number on her classroom door.

The sounds of Ecorse then and now that he remembered and appreciated were the sounds of train whistles and the trains rumbling down the tracks and the St. Francis Church bells. Boat whistles on the river—there used to be a symphony of them almost every day, especially the Bob-Lo boat—made him smile. The unwritten but scientific genealogical law of Ecorse says that almost everyone is a relative, shirttail or otherwise. Dr. McQuiston's family followed this law of Ecorse. His mother was a member of the McMurdo family, and Fergus McMurdo, an uncle of his, was killed in action in World War II. Fergus had been in the service for just thirteen months when he was killed at Graylotte, France, on November 15, 1944. He was posthumously awarded the Bronze Star. Reverend Leonard Duckett, the minister of the Ecorse Presbyterian Church when Bob was baptized and grew up in the church, officiated at the reburial of Fergus McMurdo in July 1949. His name is inscribed on a plaque on the brick wall of the Ecorse Presbyterian Church that commemorates members who were Ecorse veterans.

"I didn't get to serve myself," Dr. Bob said, a touch of regret in his voice. "I was still a tad too young." Instead, he pursued his education and, a few years later while in medical school in Iowa, his life partner Myra Dressen. After graduating from Wayne State University with a degree in chemistry, he moved to Iowa to attend the University of Des Moines, where he earned a doctor of osteopathy degree, specializing in general practice. While he lived in Des Moines away from family, friends and his home Presbyterian church, Dr. Bob attended special Sunday night programs at the Presbyterian church in Des Moines. Soon he noticed a small brunette with a sweet smile and quickly discovered that her name was Myra and that, fortunately, she was single.

The McQuistons were married in August 1953 and celebrated their fiftieth wedding anniversary in August 2003. They have three children, two daughters and a son. Beth is a nurse and Margaret a doctor with a new office in Brownstown. Son Jim and daughter-in-law Judy have given the McQuistons two grandchildren, Michael and Jim.

After returning to Ecorse in 1956, Dr. McQuiston located his office near the barbershop on Jefferson Avenue before he built his present office. He added his name to a long and distinguished list of Ecorse doctors. The 1860 census records for Ecorse revealed that in the 1860s a doctor practiced in Ecorse. His name? Dr. Comfort. In the 1920s and 1930s, some of the Ecorse doctors were Dr. Van Bessler, father and son, and Dr. Durocher. The medical roster for Dr. Bob's colleagues of the next twenty years included the names of Dr. Lee Hileman, Dr. Kembler, Dr. Sledak, Dr. Peyette, Dr. Knox, Dr. Tegnegley and Dr. Thornton. Through the years, Dr. McQuiston treated Ecorse residents both political and nonpolitical. He recalled George Coman, who was city assessor and then mayor of Ecorse from 1974 until he died in December 1975. "He fought cancer bravely," he said.

According to Dr. Bob, Dr. Lee Hileman delivered generations of Ecorse babies, and when the doctor was late or couldn't get there, often nurses like Miss Buelah Hill would help deliver babies and treat people. He envisioned a good future for doctors in Ecorse and across the country, predicting that by 2020 there will be a nationwide shortage of eighty-five thousand doctors in primary practice.

Dr. Bob had some definite ideas about Ecorse, past and future. He thought that the proliferation of shopping malls, beginning in the late 1950s, encouraged Ecorse residents to move farther out into the suburbs. He sat in his office with his diplomas in the background, counting off some of the businesses that used to flourish in Ecorse: Roth's Department Store, Slavin's Dress Shop, Ben Franklin, Affholters Dairy, Seavitt's Drug Store, Simko's Market, Kroger's, A&P and more. "Anything you wanted was within walking distance. I remember walking to the grocery store with my mother during World War II." He also remembered Ecorse Poultry Market on Jefferson where people would buy freshly killed chickens and eggs. The businesses declined when the population shifted.

Dr. Bob also attributed some of the problems of Ecorse to its rough-and-tumble politics. He remembered that Mayor Voisine founded a steel company and sold rejected steel as a good product but also recalled the positive contributions that Mayor Voisine made, including the Ecorse Public Library and the post office and helping to finance the Ecorse Boat Clubhouse. He spoke of recall elections and politicians accepting money that they shouldn't have accepted. Speaking of Larry Salisbury, the mayor of Ecorse before present Mayor Herbert W. Worthy, Dr. Bob remarked that "this mayor is moving Ecorse ahead again."

According to Dr. Bob, Ecorse and the rest of the Down River area will always have people who enjoy living along the Detroit River, even though the majority of businesses and people continue to move to the outer suburbs. "Ecorse has always had a complex, but I love it and I intend to stay here."

Then life turned the tables on Dr. Bob—he became a heart patient for a few months and died a few years later. In his case, the cliché that says that doctors are not good patients was true. "I couldn't wait to get back to work," he said. "I've had wonderful patients through the years. Ecorse has treated me very well."

Gus Gramer: Ecorse Fireman, Oarsman and Lighthouse Keeper

Newspaper reporters around the Great Lakes liked Gus Gramer, lighthouse keeper, because he gave them colorful copy. Besides making headlines by rescuing boaters from the Detroit River and Maumee Bay and pulling an oar with some of the first Ecorse Boat Club crews, Gus generated stories just by the power of his personality. His feud with Roscoe House of the Lighthouse Service provided many inches of amusing copy.

Gus developed his colorful character early in his life. Born August Gramer in New York City in 1870, he signed up with an Arctic whaling crew when he was just fifteen. In those early whaling days, single voyages lasted for years, and during these years Gus sailed the Arctic and Southern (Antarctic) Oceans. He learned the whaling trade and developed a taste for adventure that lasted him for the rest of his life.

During one of his voyages, Gus and some of his crew members were shipwrecked in the South Pacific and marooned on an island inhabited by savage native peoples. Gus vowed that if he escaped alive this would be his last whaling voyage. After arriving safely home, Gus enlisted in the United States Navy and spent the next twenty years sailing the seas for his country.

After twenty years in the navy, Gus decided that he liked the maritime life well enough to live it. He joined the U.S. Lighthouse Service and at various times in his career had charge of lighthouses on Mamajuda and Grassy Islands on the Lower Detroit River, Lightship 64 at Monroe, Michigan, and the Toledo Harbor Light in Ohio.

Mamajuda Island, which once sat in the Detroit River off of Wyandotte, Michigan, was named for an Indian woman who hunted, lived and died there, and the lighthouse that the government built on it consisted of a whitewashed frame dwelling for the keeper set on piles. Built in 1849, the tower was thirty-four feet high with a fixed red light.

When Gus moved to Grassy Island in the Lower Detroit River off Ecorse, he enjoyed the comfort of the keeper's dwelling there. The Grassy Island light tower stood twenty feet high and sat atop a frame dwelling built on piles and whitewashed. Established in 1849 as the Grassy Island Light and rebuilt in 1881, the light that Gus kept on Grassy Island was a fixed white light varied by a white flash that could be seen eleven and a half miles down the river. In the 1890s, it became the Grassy Island South Channel Range Front Light. While Gus lived in Ecorse, he became a member of the Ecorse Fire Department and rowed with the Ecorse Rowing Club.

When the Lighthouse Service transferred Gus to Lightship 64, he had to become accustomed to living on a stationary wooden scow anchored at Limekiln Crossing near Monroe in the Detroit River. Lightships 63, 64 and 65 were built in 1893 at Wyandotte, Michigan, under a government appropriation of $8,600 granted on August 5, 1892 for three small lightships in the Detroit River. Each lightship was a square-ended wooden scow, oak fastened with iron bolts and spikes, and featured a twelve-foot tripod lantern structure on the fore deck and a deckhouse aft. None of the ships was propelled. Each had a single lantern with three oil lamps hung from a twelve-foot tripod and a hand-operated bell for a fog signal. Light Vessel 64 patrolled Limekiln Crossing South from 1893 until 1910. In 1910, the United States government discontinued operating LV 64, and the Canadian government converted it into a Canadian lightship. The Canadian government replaced LV 64 in 1913 with lighted buoys.

The historical record does not pinpoint exactly the dates during which Gus operated LV 64, but it is possible to narrow down the years by process of elimination. Master Conrad Christiansen commanded LV 64 from 1895 to 1906, which means that Gus was there from 1893 to 1895 or between 1906 to 1910, when the Canadian government took over the lightship. After Gus left LV 64, he went to keep the Toledo Harbor Light, which had been built at the mouth of the Maumee River in Lake Erie off of Toledo. The Toledo Harbor had been dredged and enlarged in 1897, and the Toledo Harbor Light was built in 1904 to replace the nearby Turtle Island light that had marked the mouth of the river from 1831 to 1904. The light's main building had apartments for the keeper and two assistants and a one-story fog signal building, the cylindrical tower was thirteen feet around and the lantern measured eight feet, six inches with bar windows. The Fresnel lens, seventy-two feet above the normal water level, produced two white flashes followed by a red flash.

By the time he arrived in Toledo, Gus had earned a long life-saving record and many citations from superior officers and public officials for his bravery and efficiency. Mr. and Mrs. H.V. Deming of Toledo could attest to his life-saving skill. On May 27, 1909, the Demings were sailing in their sloop, *Red Coat*, in Maumee Bay. Suddenly, a storm swept over the sloop and capsized it. Braving a fierce gale, Gus took a small boat from the lighthouse and rowed to rescue the Demings. The waves ran so high that Gus could not get alongside the sinking *Red Coat*, so he tied one end of a rope to his boat and the other end around his body and swam to the sinking sloop. He hauled the Demings into the rowboat, rowed them to the lighthouse and took care of them until they could return to Toledo. A grateful Mrs. Deming signed over $2,000 worth of life insurance to Gus Gramer. In keeping with his nautical talents, Gus invented a grappling hook to use in deep-water dragging for bodies. He presented a pair of grappling hooks to the City of Toledo that were in service for many years.

According to Great Lakes historian Dwight Boyer, when Gus came to the Toledo Harbor Light as keeper in charge, he grappled with more than the hooks he invented. The assistant keeper at Toledo Harbor Light believed in by-the-book and proper procedures. Gus had lived his maritime life as a free spirit, rescuing and not restraining. He and the assistant keeper quarreled for weeks, their relationship as stormy as Lake Erie in one of its moods. Finally, the assistant keeper could no longer tolerate what he considered to be Gus's abrasive manner and contempt for regulations and procedures. He wrote a letter to the Lighthouse Service in Washington pouring out his anguish and charging Gus with disregard and disrespect of the Lighthouse Service.

Roscoe House, the superintendent of the Tenth Lighthouse District in Buffalo that served Lake Erie and Lake Ontario lighthouses, came to Toledo to try to mediate the quarrel between Gus and his assistant keeper. In his report of the situation in Toledo, Mr. House stated that Gus had become abusive and insolent and told him to "go to hell." Infuriated, Mr. House notified Washington of the situation in Toledo, and Washington decreed that Gus should appear at an official hearing in Toledo to explain himself. Gus neither appeared nor explained himself. The officials found Gus guilty and suspended him from the service, and Mr. House chartered a tugboat and set off for the lighthouse to tell Gus about the verdict.

Gus stubbornly refused to leave the Toledo Light and turn over all government property to his successor as he was ordered to do. Still infuriated, Mr. House returned to Toledo in the same tug he had chartered to tell Gus about his suspension, and on the next trip he made to the Toledo Harbor Light he took reinforcements. United States Marshal Wagner from Toledo and two Toledo detectives boarded the tug with Mr. House and armed themselves with pistols in case Gus decided to fight. They revisited Gus at the Toledo Harbor Light, and noting the pistols, Gus realized that his time and luck had run out. Silently, he returned with them to Toledo. As the captain and crew fixed the lines to the dock, Gus waited until a group of waiting newspapermen was within earshot. Then he roared one of his best one-liners: "Hell, you guys can't fire me…I quit!"

Music Was a Family Matter for the Campbells

Two years after he graduated, Alexander Campbell returned to Ecorse High School on Thursday, May 7, 1953, when he was the guest soloist at the annual spring Ecorse High School Band concert. He was completing his second year as member of the University of Michigan marching band and was also a member of the University's ROTC Band. He had just returned from a tour with the University of Michigan concert band.

While at Ecorse High, Alexander studied music under the direction of Herbert Saylor and was a member of the Ecorse High School Marching Band for four years. He was also one of the outstanding students in the class of 1951. At the University of Michigan he studied in the Department of Music with the intention of becoming a band director after graduation. His favorite instrument was the tenor saxophone, and he played three numbers in the Ecorse High School Band program. They were "Concerto No. 1," by Singeless, "Concertina" by Guilhaud and "Tambourin" by Rameau. Mrs. Doris Green accompanied him at the piano.

Both the Ecorse Senior High Band and the sixty-piece Junior High Band appeared in the musical program, which featured both standard music and popular numbers.

After playing with his old band, Alexander returned to the University of Michigan and played more solos. In 1954, he and other students competed in the annual Gulantics talent show in Hill Auditorium. His trio, headed by Anceo Franciso on piano with Jimmie Williams on bass, took the twenty-five-dollar third-place prize.

"I played in the Michigan Band under William Revelli—who was a great man, he made me sweat blood—but I also led a popular jazz sextet," Alexander later recalled. He graduated from the School of Music with a BA in 1955 and a master's degree in 1960. He once again returned to Ecorse High School, where he directed the band for thirty years until he retired to California with his wife Barbara in 1986.

Alexander Campbell, his wife and their sons, Alexander T., Garland and David, were also musicians. Alexander T. played sax in the University of Michigan Band from 1975 to 1977, and David (the youngest) played percussion while getting his BA in fine arts in 1980. Garland earned his University of Michigan degree in political science and communications and was an Emmy-winning producer of children's TV programs before becoming a college band director.

Garland said that having a band director for a father meant that he and his brothers "always had all sorts of instruments at home—violins, guitars, trombones. We learned something about all of them because they were sitting around the house. My mom was a musician, too, but she became an occupational therapist."

"We didn't cram anything down their throats, but we exposed them to opportunities I wish I'd had. I used to pack them up, leave home and take them to Ann Arbor to listen to the Michigan Band practice," Alexander Sr. said.

The Ecorse High School Band marched in the Mardi Gras Parade in New Orleans on February 29, 1976. The appearance of the seventy-nine-member band in the four-and-a-half-hour parade marked the first time that a unit from Michigan or from the North appeared in the parade, which is the final celebration before Lent.

The band members, director Campbell, assistant director Jerry Copeland and thirteen chaperones boarded three buses from Ecorse High School the Friday before the parade. Many Ecorse residents gathered at the school to see them off. Mrs. Marie Salisbury—an Ecorse resident for twenty-three years and mother of Larry Salisbury, a school board member at the time—obtained the invitation for the band to participate in the parade. Mrs. Salisbury had attended Mardi Gras for the past seventeen years and had "never seen a Michigan group participate." A family friend, Arthur Daure, was chairman of the Krewe of Thoth parade and it was from him that she received the invitation to invite any group she wished. "I could have invited any civic group of older people, but I thought it would be better to give those youngsters a chance to make good on the invitation."

The band members and their families and friends raised $13,000 through various projects, including bake sales, a spaghetti dinner and lunch, a hockey benefit, a card party, a paper drive, a band concert, a student dance, a candle sale and a medallion sale. Many civic organizations, business leaders and private citizens also assisted. The largest contribution came from the City of Ecorse, which gave $2,600 for a bus rental.

Co-chairmen of the parents' committee were Mrs. Rhoda Daunter and Mrs. Lorraine Lewis. Student leaders were Pete Martinez, chairman, Sheryl Copeland and Andrea Beard.

Ecorse People

Herbert Saylor and Alexander Campbell directed the Ecorse High School Band and created warm memories for generations of Ecorse musicians.

The Ecorse High School Band was a marching machine that provided precision drills and beautiful music for Ecorse events and school concerts.

Alexander Sr. played sax for Motown records during the company's heyday with Martha and the Vandellas, the Temptations, the Four Tops and other groups. In the fall of 1996 the Campbells released their first album from Square 1 produced by their company, Bunk Bed Music, and marketed by another family firm, Marquis Records of Wilmington, California. Alexander Sr. was the session director for the recording, and three other musicians completed the Campbell Brothers sextet.

Fire Chief Milton Montie and Ecorse Grew Up Together

Fire Chief Milton Montie had the distinction of being the last person to be employed by the Village of Ecorse. He was appointed to the fire department on January 19, 1942, and Ecorse officially became a city on January 27, 1942, when the city charter was adopted.

Milton was born into both a pioneer Ecorse family and a firefighting tradition. His father was an Ecorse firefighter in the 1920s when the city's firemen were also policemen. "I used to hang around there all of the time," he recalled.

Benjamin, Milton's father, was killed in a shootout with bank robbers at Robber's Roost on the Ecorse waterfront in 1924. "Chief Albert Jaeger killed the bank robber that shot my father," Milton recalled when telling the story. He recited details down to the names of the robbers.

A year after he joined the Ecorse Fire Department, Milton entered the army, in which he was one of a thirty-seven-man detachment that landed in Italy with the infantry. For nearly two years he served as senior officer of a group that extinguished fires at major seaports and supply depots throughout Italy and North Africa. Milton served in the army until December 1, 1945, and then returned to his job with the Ecorse Fire Department.

During the next decade, Milton moved up the ranks in the Ecorse Fire Department. He became sergeant in April 1950, lieutenant in May 1957, acting assistant chief in February 1964 and assistant chief in April 1964. On September 3, 1974, he became fire chief.

Three Ecorse fires blaze in the chief's memory: the Union Carbide fire in 1961 involving an oxygen explosion that killed three people; the Linde Air Company fire of 1962, and the Chase Apartments fire of 1972, where six people died. He considered these fires the worst in Ecorse history. "We spent five days looking for bodies after the Chase Apartments fire," he remembered.

Personally, he said that he had a few close calls. "There was that fire in a plastics factory at 256 Salliotte. Everything was going fine, and then there was this big explosion. If I'd been 20 feet closer, I'd be dead." But the chief was fortunate. His only serious injury came while he was fighting a coal fire in which he burnt his foot severely.

During his years with the Ecorse Fire Department, Milton was a member of the Arson Squad, a training officer and civil defense liaison, taking an active part in civil defense work since 1951. He was an outspoken advocate of fire prevention and revived the annual Fire Prevention Week programs in the public schools.

In 1966, Milton received the distinguished service award for civic services from the Ecorse Kiwanis Club. He could usually be called on to head up functions and civic activities. In July 1977, he was chairman of the successful Ecorse Water Festival.

In 1977, Milton decided to retire, since the Ecorse Fire Department required firemen to retire at sixty and his sixtieth birthday was on September 3, 1977. "I was thinking about retiring July 11, then decided against it. I decided to hand in my resignation today," he said in the third week of July.

The day of Milton's retirement, Ecorse Police and Fire Commissioner Roosevelt (Rudy) Lackey reminisced with the chief in his office. Lackey said, "He will be missed by many. I hope we can fill the position with a man in his footsteps." Deputy Fire Chief Jim Clemons was appointed to be acting fire chief until the position was filled.

As for now civilian Milton Montie, he planned to take a vacation at his cottage near the Au Sable River in northern Michigan. After that, he said, "Well, I'd like to keep working the fire prevention field. I've been so active for so long I can't keep still."

Photo by John Duguay

John Duguay proudly says that he first picked up a camera when he was just seven years old, and he has had a camera (perhaps not the same one!) in his hand since then.

The years between John's first camera in the early 1920s and his most recent pictures have been eventful ones. After being educated in Ecorse and Detroit schools, he worked for a time at an Ecorse company and Ford Motor Company, and then he joined the navy in 1942 and served for three years. John counts a Bronze Star as one of the decorations that he won for his service as a demolitions expert and a Navy Seal during World War II. The citation for his Bronze Star reads:

> *For distinguishing himself by meritorious achievement in February 1945, as a member of an assault unit during the assault and capture of Iwo Jima Island. In the face of enemy rifle, machine gun, and mortar fire, he bravely prepared the way for the operations of combat troops and by his courageous devotion to duty contributed greatly to the success of this hazardous mission. His*
>
> *courage and conduct throughout were in keeping with the best traditions of the naval service.*
>
> *—R.K. Turner, Admiral, U.S. Navy*

After John returned to Ecorse, he went to work for several local companies as an assembly line designer, and while he was working on one of his projects, a piece of metal flew up and pierced his eye, causing him to lose sight in it. John didn't let this accident slow him down. He continued to design assembly lines and set up a photography studio in his basement. His photos regularly appeared in local publications, including the *Ecorse Advertiser*. John's pictures are a visual chronicle and an important part of the documentary record of Ecorse history.

Maria Gokey, Queen of Ecorse

Memories of the Depression days in Ecorse are still fresh in the mind of Maria Gokey of Eighth Street. She recalls the sounds and smells and work of planting a spring garden with seeds donated by Henry Ford. She and her family staked out the nearest vacant lot and raked and weeded it by hand. Then they planted the cabbage, zucchini, corn, hot pepper seeds and tomato plants and watched them grow. "Only we couldn't watch them too long because we had other chores to do," she says with a laugh.

When it came time to harvest the garden, her mother put Maria and her brother and sisters to work. Her mother and father had immigrated to the United States as migrant farm workers from Mexico and worked their way through Texas and other states before they settled in Ypsilanti, where Maria was born. They came to Ecorse in 1929. Maria remembers another of her early childhood chores was making tortillas in the morning to take to school for lunch. One of the important chores that Maria and her three brothers performed every day was walking along the railroad tracks picking up coal for the heating and cooking stoves. It was also Maria's job to haul a bucket of water to heat on the fire outside for doing dishes and washing. "We knew how to work from an early age," she says.

A house on High and First Streets by the railroad tracks was one of the first places in which Maria and her family lived, and during the Depression they entertained many unexpected visitors from along the trades. One time, two men came down the tracks and asked Maria's mother if they could work for a sandwich. "I have no work, but I'll give you your supper," Maria's mother told the men. She gave them a sandwich of beans and tortillas.

The Prohibition years, 1920–33, were also interesting times to live through in Ecorse. Maria recalls that one of the Ecorse officials—without getting any more specific, a man by the name of Riopelle—bought her mother all of the equipment needed to make beer and delivered it to their house. Her mother made the beer, which everyone enjoyed for twenty-five cents per glass, and their guests entertained everyone by pumping the player piano, which Mr. Riopelle also supplied. When federal customs agents came around hunting bootleg liquor, Maria's parents would bury it under a pile of straw in the barn with rabbit cages on top of it.

Maria remembers rowing over to Fighting Island in a small boat and taking a river cruise in one of the tour boats that plied the Down River waterfront in 1956. "I was standing there waiting for the boat, and my cousin thought I looked so pretty and thoughtful that she snapped my picture," Maria laughs.

After moving away from Ecorse for a brief time, Maria returned and immediately became actively involved in the community. She spent forty active years in the Ecorse Veterans of Foreign Wars Post 5709, serving as president in the 1970s, and she proudly displays a plaque from the Down River Latin American Club recognizing her "31 years of loyal service." She also gave twenty years of loyal service to General Motors before she retired in 1993.

Maria raised a family of four daughters and a son, which has expanded to nineteen grandchildren, twenty-four great-grandchildren and one great-great-grandchild. Her family recently threw her an eightieth birthday party, and the Ecorse mayor and city council presented her with a plaque proclaiming her an outstanding Ecorse citizen. Her friends and fellow parishioners at St. Francis Xavier Church call her "La Reina," Spanish for "the Queen of Ecorse."

Maria displays her pride at being an American citizen by flying a fifty-year-old American flag from her house on Memorial Day and the Fourth of July. "This country has given me my life and so has Ecorse. I want to give back all I can."

Ecorse People

Cub Scouts in Ecorse earned badges and did much community service.

Kidettes enjoyed marching in Ecorse parades and other celebrations.

African Americans in Ecorse contributed drum majors and majorettes to its marching bands.

The girls' drill team added precision and pulchritude to Ecorse parades.

For decades, the Ecorse Recreation Department sponsored sports and activities for Ecorse citizens. An indoor hockey rink was an important part of the program.

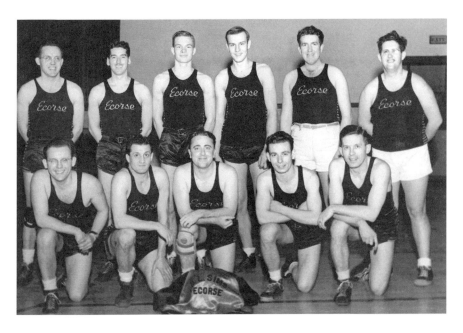

Basketball is another important Ecorse sport.

Many Ecorse boys and girls learned the rules of skating and good sportsmanship at the hockey rink.

The Presbyterian Church and other organizations sponsored several Girl Scout troops in Ecorse.

Ecorse People

Besides hockey, Ecorse children and adults enjoyed ice skating at the Ecorse Ice Rink.
Before it was enclosed, skaters would circle around the open-air rink and enjoy hot
chocolate breaks.

Hockey banquets were an important recognition of the prowess of the hockey teams.

Since 1929, Great Lakes Steel played a pivotal role in Ecorse History, and the Great Lakes Steel Management Club focused on improving the community.

The Ecorse Jaycees actively promoted businesses and contributed to the well-being of the community.

Ecorse Goodfellows worked together to make sure that everyone in Ecorse had a good Christmas.

The Ecorse Rotary and Kiwanis Clubs represented the growth of business and the good of community in Ecorse.

Chartered in 1940, the Downriver Pennsylvania Club practiced a community and charity outreach until it disbanded in 2003.

Before it was transformed into a hockey arena, the municipal skating rink in Ecorse was a favorite skating spot for generations of Ecorse citizens.

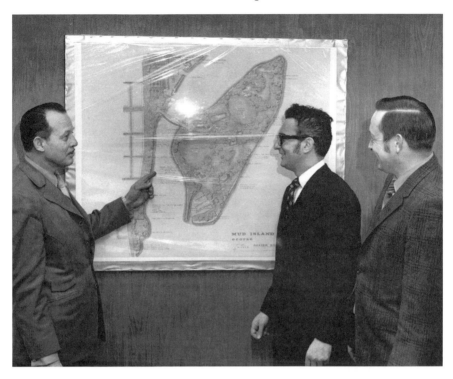

Above: In 1965, Mayor Albert B. Buday and the Ecorse City Council attempted to cut Mud Island down to size so that riverfront visitors could enjoy the Detroit River's many maritime activities.

Right: Fishing on the Detroit River has always been a popular and productive sport.

The Detroit and Ecorse Rivers have shaped the maritime history of Ecorse and the other Down River communities.

An electric car was a fun addition to the Ecorse water festivals and parades.

The Ecorse Water Festival of 1966 featured cars, the Ecorse High School Band, floats and veterans groups.

A Fourth of July Festival and parade have been important Ecorse traditions for generations.

The Roy B. Salliotte Post #319 of the American Legion has entered a float in nearly every Ecorse parade.

Ecorse has had several dens of Cub Scouts over the years.

The Hispanic or Latino population of Ecorse represents about 8.94 percent of the population, but their influence in civic and community affairs is much larger than their numbers would suggest.

Along with other Ecorse mayors, Mayor Richard Manning had a special place in his heart for senior citizens and daily activities.

Ecorse senior citizens enjoy their community events.

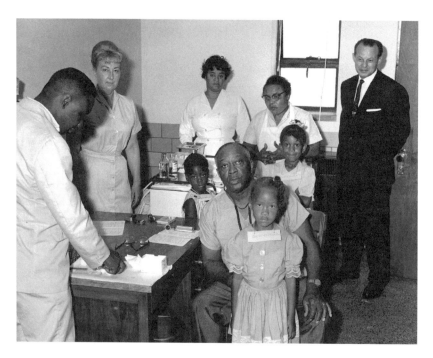

Dr. Jerry A. Thornton (seated) became the city physician of Ecorse in 1945 and served until he died in 1979.

BIBLIOGRAPHY

Manuscripts

Anderson, Thomas J. "A History of Southgate and Detroit Downriver Area." Southgate, Michigan. October 1963.

Burton Historical Collections. Detroit Public Library. Detroit, Michigan.

City of Ecorse Election Precinct Maps, 1957. Ecorse City Hall.

Hammang, John M., PhD. "Sovereignty and Title in Detroit's Downriver." 2004.

Historical Collections of the Great Lakes. Bowling Green State University Archives. Bowling Green, Ohio.

Wayne County Plats, courtesy of Mrs. Rita Heller. Located in the Wayne County Courthouse.

Periodicals

Down River magazine. Down River Chamber of Commerce, Southgate, Michigan, 1959.

Local Government Data Book for Michigan, 1962.

Newspapers

Detroit Free press
Detroit News
Ecorse Advertiser

Ecorse Tribune
Mellus Newspapers

Books

Bald, F. Clever. *Detroit's First American Decade: 1796–1805*. Ann Arbor: University of Michigan Press, 1948.

———. *Michigan in Four Centuries*. New York: Harper & Row, Publishers, 1954.

Brown, Gerald S., Hugh Keenleyside and W.P.M. Kennedy. *Canada and the United States: Some Aspects of their Historical Relations*. New York: Alfred A. Knopf, 1952.

Burton, Clarence. *History of Wayne County*. Vols. 1–4. Chicago: S.J. Clarke Publishing Company, 1930.

Calloway, Colin G. *The American Revolution in Indian Country*. New York: Cambridge University Press, 1998.

Caton, Bruce. *Michigan: A Bicentennial History*. New York: W.W. Norton & Company, 1976.

Danziger, Edmund Jefferson, Jr. *Survival and Regeneration: Detroit's American Indian Community*. Detroit, MI: Wayne State University Press, 1991.

DeWindt, Mrs. Joseph (Edwina). *Proudly We Record, Wyandotte*. Wyandotte, MI: Rotary Club of Wyandotte, 1955.

Eckert, Allan. *Wilderness Empire*. New York: Bantam Books, 1969.

Engelmann, Larry. *Intemperance*. New York: The Free Press, 1979.

Farmer, Silas. *History of Detroit and Michigan*. Detroit, MI: self-published, 1890.

Finlay, J.L., and D.N. Sprague. *The Structure of Canadian History*. Fourth Edition. Toronto, ON: Prentice Hall, 1993.

Gilpin, Alec R. *The Territory of Michigan: 1805–1837*. East Lansing: Michigan State University Press, 1970.

Gordon, Mitchell. *Sick Cities: Psychology and Pathology of American Urban Life*. Baltimore, MD: Penguin Books, 1969.

Hartig, John, ed. *Honoring Our Detroit River, Caring For Our Home*. Bloomfield Hills, MI: Cranbrook Institute of Science, 2003.

Havighust, Walter. *Flags at the Straits: The Forts of Mackinac*. Englewood Cliffs, NJ: Prentice-Hall, Inc., 1966.

Horsman, Reginald. *The Causes of the War of 1812*. Philadelphia: University of Pennsylvania Press, 1962.

Illustrated Historical Atlas of Wayne County. Detroit, MI: H. Belden & Company, 1876.

Innis, Harold A. *The Fur Trade in Canada*. New Haven, CT: Yale University Press, 1962.

Jacobson, Judy. *Detroit River Connections: Historical and Biographical Sketches of the Eastern Great Lakes Border Region*. Baltimore, MD: Genealogical Publishing Company, 1994.

Jennings, Francis. *The Invasion of America: Indians, Colonialism, and the Cant of Conquest*. Williamsburg, VA: Institute of American History and Culture, 1976.

Louder, Dean R., and Eric Waddell, eds. *French America: Mobility, Identity, and Minority Experience Across the Continent*. Baton Rouge: Louisiana State University Press, 1983.

Mackay, Douglas. *The Honourable Company: A History of the Hudson's Bay Company*. Toronto, ON: McClelland & Stewart, 1949.

Mansfield, J.B. *History of the Great Lakes, Illustrated in Two Volumes*. Vols 1–2. Chicago: J.H. Beers & Co., 1899. Reprinted by Freshwater Press, Cleveland, OH, 1972.

Murphy, Lucy Eldersveld. *A Gathering of Rivers: Indians, Metis, and Mining in the Western Great Lakes, 1737–1832.* Lincoln: University of Nebraska Press, 2000.

Nowlin, William. *The Bark Covered House.* Ann Arbor, MI: University Microfilms, Inc., 1876.

Nute, Grace Lee. *The Voyageur.* Reprint Edition. St. Paul: Minnesota Historical Society, 1955.

Parkins, Almon Ernest. *The Historical Geography of Detroit.* New York: Port Washington, 1970.

Peck, Anne Merriman. *The Pageant of Canadian History.* Toronto, ON: Longmans, Green and Company, 1943.

Polk's Detroit Directory 1929. University of Michigan "M" Library, Ann Arbor, Michigan.

Prucha, Francis Paul. *Broadax and Bayonet: The Role of the United States Army in the Development of the Northwest, 1815–1850.* Lincoln: University of Nebraska Press, 1995.

Quaife, Milo Milton, ed., Secretary of the Burton Historical Collection. *War on the Detroit: The Chronicles of Thomas Vercheres de Boucherville and the Capitulation by an Ohio Volunteer.* Chicago: Lakeside Press, R.R. Donnelley & Sons Co., 1940.

Robertson, Jno, Adjutant General. *Michigan in the War.* Lansing, MI: W.S. George & Co., State Printers and Binders, 1880.

Russell, Nelson Vance. *The British Regime in Michigan and the Old Northwest: 1769-1796.* Philadelphia, PA: Porcupine Press, 1978.

Skaggs, David Curtis, and William Jeffrey Welsh. "War on the Great Lakes: Essays Commemorating the 175th Anniversary of the Battle of Lake Erie." War on the Great Lakes Symposium. Kent, OH: Kent State University Press, 1991.

Skaggs, David Curtis, and Larry L. Nelson, eds. *The Sixty Years' War for the Great Lakes, 1754–1814*. East Lansing: Michigan State University Press, 2001.

The Story of Ste. Anne de Detroit Church, Detroit, Michigan: 1701–1976 and the Bicentennial History of Catholic America. South Hackensack, NJ: Custom Books, Inc., 1976.

Talman, James J. *Basic Documents in Canadian History*. Toronto, ON: D. Van Nostrand Company, Inc. 1959.

Tucker, Glenn. *Paltroons and Patriots: A Popular Account of the War of 1812*, Vols. 1–2. Indianapolis, IN: Bobbs-Merrill, 1954.

Vogel, Virgil J. *Indian Names in Michigan*. Ann Arbor. University of Michigan Press, 1986.

Vorderstresse, Alfred B. *Detroit in the War of 1812*. Detroit, MI: Wayne State University Press, 1951.

White, Richard. *The Middle Ground: Indians, Empires, and Republics in the Great Lakes Region, 1650–1815*. New York: Cambridge University Press, 1991.

Williams, Frederick D. *Michigan Soldiers in the Civil War*. Bureau of History. Lansing: Michigan Department of State, 1988.

Woodford, Frank B., and Albert Hyman. Detroit, MI: Wayne State University Press, 1958.

ABOUT THE AUTHOR

Kathy Covert Warnes was born in the old Wyandotte General Hospital on the banks of the Detroit River. Ecorse and the Detroit and Ecorse Rivers flowing around it were such foundational parts of her childhood that she took them for granted. Like a long, lazy summer day at Bob-Lo Island, she thought that the rivers would always be there, waiting for her to revisit them when she needed to do so. Then life dictated that she and the rivers would move in different directions. She didn't get to college until she was in her thirties. Busy trying to earn a living and raise her daughter by herself, she eventually went on to earn her PhD in history in 2006 and has just completed a three-year visiting professorship in history at Grand Valley State University.

Visit us at
www.historypress.net